POLITICAL SCIENCE - INTRODUCTION TO AMERICAN GOVERNMENT

The American Democracy in History and Context

Klaus Labuttis

Klaus Labuttis

Foreword

~

This Book is the compilation and result of my teaching the Government Constitution portion of California State University Title 5, Section 40404 at Yuba College, California.

This Book has risen from my teaching notes and is broken down to the most essential information and aspects of this mandatory College course.

It shall be considered the minimum knowledge you need in your Political Science Introduction Class to master any required essays or exams.

I wish you good luck in your studies, and may the facts provided here stimulate you for any further readings.

Klaus Labuttis
Oregon House, California

Introduction
This Book Intention

This Book Intention

With this Book, you have all important information available, to pass any test or write any essay for your College required Political Science Course 1 "Introduction to American Government".

Each chapter gives you the facts and highlights that matters within the topic. The compactness of the information and easy explanations prepare you to succeed in this class.

This Book is much more to the point than any other of the

available literature on this subject. Having taught this course myself, I feel confident that you will have a very direct and comprehensive approach to the topic of American Government. This text is written for you to succeed and to know the fundamentals.

Regarding Tests

Remember that this is a historical political course, so you need to know the basic historic outline. See the developments today in their historical context and relate the words of the Constitution to previous and current interpretations.

This Book covers the required three parts of American Government and Politics:

1. The Foundations of American Democracy, including the Constitution, Civil Liberties, and Civil Rights.

2. The powerful political forces like media, political parties, elections, and interest groups.

3. Political Institutions, like Congress, the Presidency, the Federal Bureaucracy. State and Local Governments.

At the end of the Book you will understand the structure and principals of the U.S Government and the Constitution. You will know what defines a democracy and understand the balance of power between the various branches of government.

IMPORTANT

The information in this Book will help you to satisfy the Government(s) Constitution(s) portion of California State University Title 5, Section 40404.

This Course material is written for you to understand easily difficult concepts in the US-American democratic process. The information shall help you to answer topic related questions in a simple and yet academic way.

I will point out important aspects and elements within the topic of each chapter. This will allow you to focus on questions and connections, that for sure will appear in tests and essay questions.

Always remember that Political Science lives from discussing a topic with its different aspects and not being shy to question traditions and habits.

As a "good student" you need to have an opinion, do not hesitate to ask a confronting question or offer a different take on a subject. Every teacher will appreciate this and will strive to explain his or her position while thanking you internally.

Some important points to keep in mind, before we begin:

- We are the world's oldest electoral democracy. Specific traditions have been developed in limiting the government's power, the rule of law and the free operating opposition.
- The economic prosperity is a major factor in the successful development of democratic institutions.
- Politic governs our lives. Politicians shape our society and the laws they ratify influence us profoundly.

Chapter 1

Founding and The Constitution

~

YOU NEED TO KNOW

The American government is an institution born out of reason and reflection

At its foundation lie three historic documents:

- the Declaration of Independence (1776)
- the Constitution (1788)
- the Bill of Rights (1791)

<u>**Please note**</u>

Many stories and anecdotes about the "Framers" or "Founding Fathers" are important, because it shows their different approaches for the new democracy.

Different interest groups tried to strengthen their position in the negotiations. British traditions were incorporated as well as revolutionary ideas of 'dividing power' and the focus on individual freedom.

Principles of American Government

While political leaders, movements and interpretations have come and gone in the past 200 years, the underlying principles of American government have remained the same.

Declaration of Independence

Includes Unalienable Rights:
    <u>Liberty - Freedom - Pursuit of Happiness</u>

Constitution

Establishes the 3 branches of government – legislative, executive and judicial
    Creates "checks and balances"
    Basic Freedoms: Freedom to speak, Freedom to assemble peacefully, Freedom to worship, Freedom from government intrusion

Bill of Rights

Symbolizes the Ideal of the American Government
The first ten Amendments to the Constitution

Key Concepts and Time Reference

1

<u>The work of political philosophers influenced the Founders</u>

Thomas Hobbes and John Locke: "The idea of a social contract that holds the government accountable by the people and bound to protect the natural right of its citizens."
Montesquieu: "Separation of power"

2

<u>Articles of Confederation (1781 to 1788)</u>

Like United Nations (UN): every state had virtually all-governmental powers
Congress without power: Representatives sent from states, no money
"The first constitution of the United States guaranteeing the state's sovereignty over all issues. A weak central government with no power to enforce unity."

<u>Definition:</u>
Confederation = a union of independent states whose central

government is charged with few powers where upon the states keep their power intact.

3

The 'new' Constitution of 1787 combined selfish interests and high principle

The Constitution was the product of consensus, conflict and compromise

Three-Fifth Compromise (each slave counts as 3/5 of a person)
Great Compromise creates bicameral system. A lower house (later House of Representatives) and upper house (later Senate)

THE CONSTITUTION

<u>To remember:</u>

3 months of fierce debating
Majority of the 12 state delegations supported it, signed on September 17th 1787

Four Core Principles

1

<u>Republicanism</u>

Power rests with the people, but the people rule indirectly

Talking Point:
How much democracy did the framers wanted?

2

Federalism

Power is divided between the central and state governments
Difference to confederation and unitary system
Constitution lists powers of the national government and it
lists the powers denied to the states; implying that all other powers
were retained by the states
See later 10th Amendment – Important is <u>Supremacy Clause</u>
in Article VI, Section 2, stating that the Constitution is the
supreme law of the land

3

Separation of Powers

Power is divided across all three co-equal branches of government
Preventing concentration of power. Difference to
Parliamentary System

4

Checks and Balances

Power is both divided and shared among the 3 branches
(legislative, executive, judicial)

Each branch or government institution has some control over
the other two

A method to protect against unrestraint governmental power

Articles of the Constitution

There is a total of 7 articles, preceded by a preamble and followed
by the Amendments

They were first 10 Amendments, the so called "Bill of Rights";
currently we have 27 Amendments or Additions to the
Constitution

<u>Preamble</u>

The fundamental goal is establishing justice and 'securing the
blessings of Liberty'

It starts with: "We the people ..."

The Constitution gave new powers to the national
government

<u>Legislative</u>

The Framers thought this branch of government as the most
important and therefore named it first

"All legislative power herein granted shall be vested in a Congress ... which consists of a Senate and a House of Representatives."

The Powers of Congress given by the Constitution fall into two broad categories: enumerated and implied powers

Enumerated Powers

Specifically listed powers in Article1, Section 8:

- Impose and collect taxes
- Borrow money
- Regulate commerce
- Coin money
- Impose duties
- Controls federal appropriations (budget)
- Approves treaties and presidential appointments
- Regulates interstate commerce
- Establishes lower court systems

Implied Powers

Are those authorized by the

Elastic Clause (also called "necessary" and "proper" clause), Art. 1, Sec. 8

These are powers that are not named in the Constitution, but are "implied", meaning that these powers follow either an interpretation of the articles or have evolved out of tradition

This very important aspect of the Constitution provides the Congress with a source of strength. It provides Congress with the authority to make all laws necessary

Executive

Art II of the Constitution defines the Executive authority and gives the President the authority to carry out laws

Important: Sec1, "...takes care that the Laws be faithfully executed"
> This means that the executive power is vested in the president
> Laws need to be interpreted and executed and it is up to the executive branch to do so

Enumerated Powers

In Article II, Section 2 the powers of the President are defined
> Commander in Chief
> Foreign Treaties, proposes laws, pardons
> Appoints Supreme Court justices and federal court judges

<u>Judicial</u>

Article III of the Constitution is the shortest of all. It establishes a Supreme Court and implies that the judges will have a life tenure.

<u>Request for Congress to establish a lower court system:</u>
Done in 1789 through the Judiciary Act

<u>Supreme Court</u>

Reviews lower court decisions
Constitutionality of laws = judicial review
Decides disputes between states

The **judicial review** is not written into the Constitution. It is a right assumed by the Supreme Court stemming out of a Supreme Court Decision Mulberry versus Madison. This decision is an important milestone for the importance, the court plays today

Articles IV to VII

These articles cover a wide range of issues:

<u>Article IV</u> declares

States need to give "full faith and credit" to the laws of the other states

Prohibiting discrimination by one state against citizens of another

<u>Article V</u> spells out the amendment process

<u>Article VI</u> defines the Supremacy Clause:

stating that no religious test can be performed to qualify an applicant for any office.

<u>Article VII</u> contains the ratifying Constitution procedures

<u>Ratifying the Constitution</u>

The new Constitution was highly controversial

Federalists (James Madison) against Antifederalists (George Mason)

<u>Federalists</u>

Believed that elites were best to govern, 'filtration'

Favored strong national government

<u>Antifederalists</u>

Government should be closer to the people
    No concentration of power
    Strong focus on individual rights

Checks and Balances

Later constitutional amendments dramatically changed the
relationship between Americans and their government:

Bill of Rights

1868 Slaves become fully citizens
    Senators directly elected (before appointed by state legislators)
    27 Amendments so far

To propose an Amendment

Two-thirds of both houses of Congress vote to propose an
amendment
    or
    Two thirds of the state legislatures ask Congress to call a
national convention to propose amendments

To ratify an Amendment

Three-fourths of the state legislatures approve it
	or
	Ratifying conventions in three-fourths of the states approve it

<u>Tidbit:</u>
Only the first proposal method has been used and the first form of ratification except the twenty first Amendment, Prohibition.

<u>Important Amendments:</u>

Amendment 13: Eliminated slavery – 1865

Amendment 15: Extended voting rights to all races – 1869

Amendment 16: Income Tax – 1913

Amendment 19: Women can vote – 1920

Amendment 26: Voting age is 18 years – 1971

Chapter 2

Federalism

~

YOU NEED TO KNOW

- In our system of government (federalism), the federal and state governments share power
- Under federalism, the functions of government are divided
- The federal government has exclusive domain over international affairs and national defense
- Other matters such as education, crime control, housing, and taxes, fall within the province of both the federal and state governments
- There is a healthy tension between the federal and state governments over the roles and responsibilities of each

Sovereignty in the American Political System

Located nowhere – sovereignty is shared in complicated ways and is 'ever changing'

The power balance depends on public law domain and on the period of history

Talking Points:

Why is the question of "Who should do what" very important in American politics?

The federal government is setting national standards to limit inequality across the states. Is this concept working?

Key Concepts

Federalism has shaped American politics from the country's beginning

The Constitution reflects the disputes between Federalist-Antifederalist, leading to the Bill of Rights

The definition of federalism has changed radically in the last two centuries

Definitions

Federal System

Power is formally divided between national government and regional entities

Confederal System

System of government in which power rests primarily with regional entities that have bonded together to form a league of independent governments

Unitary System

National government has ultimate control over all areas of policy

National Powers

The **elastic clause** also called <u>necessary and proper clause</u> gives Congress the power to create laws ensuring the power of the national government

The <u>supremacy clause</u> in the Constitution makes sure that all laws must be congruent with its statues ("the law of the land")

Several Amendments to the Constitution included the <u>enabling clause</u>, giving Congress power to enforce the provisions of the Amendment

Enumerated Powers

These are domains of the national government that are directly expressed in the Constitution

- Tax, borrow and coin money
- Regulate interstate commerce
- Declare war
- Provide for army and navy
- Make naturalization laws
- Create system of federal courts

State Powers

Defined in the Tenth Amendment

"The powers not delegated to the United States by the Constitution, nor prohibited by it to the States, are reserved to the States respectively, or to the people"

Delegated powers are the enumerated and implied powers of Congress

Subtract these delegated powers plus any power that the Constitution prohibits states from having, then you are left with the reserved powers to the states

Prohibited Powers

States cannot sign treaties or coin money

State Powers

- Provide for public health, safety and morality
- Coercion = develop and enforce criminal codes
- Regulate commerce within state
- Establish local governments
- Ratify amendments to the constitution
- Determine voter qualification
- Conduct elections

Concurrent Powers (Shared Powers)

Levy taxes

For example, states cannot impose import taxes, only the federal government can. Real Estate tax is state tax. Taxes on payroll and gasoline are taxed from both

Borrow money
Charter banks and corporations
Establish courts

State governments are structured similarly to the federal government. Every state has their own state constitution and has established three branches of government with a bicameral system

<u>State Constitution</u>

No two states are alike and often-good policies, procedures and laws are copied from another

Every state has a constitution, but it is 'subordinate' to the supreme law of the land

Alabama's constitution has 172,000 words, Vermont's less than 7000 words

California's constitution mandates the seizes of fruit boxes Oklahoma's mandates to teach agriculture in public schools

<u>Governor</u>

Governor is the highest elected official, modeled after the presidency

Launching pad for a national office, 23 governors served as president or vice president, but 1 governor became a taxi driver and another a bank teller

First woman governor in Wyoming 1925 (Mrs. Ross)

First and only black governor in Virginia 1989 (Mr. Wilder)

$140,000 salary in California, $60,000 in Arkansas

New Jersey governor constitutionally strongest, Texas governor weakest, but all are chief of "National Guard"

Governor drafts annual budget and then state legislatures negotiate back and forth to get it into law

<u>State Legislators</u>

Part time job in some states like Alabama. In other states, like California and New York, legislators receive 90,000 plus salaries

New Hampshire has 400 legislators for 1Million residents. New Jersey has 120 legislators for 6 Million citizens

Normally two chambers (named also Senate and House of Representative); Nebraska is the exception with only one chamber

The Process of passing legislation is copied from the national Congress

There are five major areas of legislation

1

Education

Includes state universities

Local municipalities are responsible for primary and secondary schools.

Talking Point:

What means the "no child left behind" policy and is it successful?

2

Roads and Highways

Speed limits, DMV, infrastructure repairs

3

<u>Health and Welfare</u>

A very large area of state responsibility. Includes state hospitals, unemployment insurance, welfare benefits. States regulate medical professionals and care centers.

4

<u>Law and Order</u>

State Highway Patrol and State Police

5

<u>Conservation Efforts</u>

Parks, public land, regulating fishing and hunting

Positions

<u>Lieutenant Governor</u>

This position is the "vice president" to the governor. Some states do elect the lieutenant governor separately, like in Texas.

Attorney General

The attorney general is the highest legal officer in the state.

Talking Point:
Discuss the Independence of the Justice Department

Reapportionment and Redistricting

Constitution requires that the national government conducts a census every 10 year

Census is the basis to reapportion (reassign) Congressional seats. It is up to state legislator to redraw Congressional seats

"Gerrymandering" = redrawing congressional districts for delivering a partisan advantage to one party

Relationship among States

The full faith and credit clause requires each state to give "full Faith and Credit ... to the public Acts, Records, and judicial Proceedings of every state

The privileges and immunities clause forbids a state from denying citizens of other states the rights it confers to its own citizens

The extradition clause deals with someone who is charged with a crime in one state, but who flees justice

With the consent of Congress, the states can enter interstate compacts and agreements

Competing Interpretations of Federalism

There are in general two divergent views of how to interpret the Constitution regarding Federalism

Dual Federalism

This interpretation of the Constitution favors state rights by claiming that it was a contract between existing states. These states willingly gave certain powers to the national government, but retained all other powers not specifically delegated

The dual federalist also request to read the Constitution as a "fixed" document and does not allow changing interpretation

Cooperative Federalism

Cooperative Federalism favors the national government as superior to the states. For the cooperative federalist – a term from the New Deal of the 1930s – the Constitution is a contract between people and not states. For them the Constitution is a living document and Congress can use the necessary and proper clause in a very broad way

Meaning and Change in Federalism

Federalism and its interpretation has changed many times in American History due to the rulings of the Supreme Court. At times the states were more empowered, but overall the strengthening of the federal government has taken place.

1

Cooperative Federalism (1801 -1835 under Chief Justice John Marshall)

McCulloch versus Maryland (1819): Baltimore Branch of the Bank of the United States cannot be taxed and Congress has the right to create a national bank

Gibbons versus Ogden (1824): ruling in favor of broad national power in relation to commerce clause in the Constitution. A federal license is as powerful as a state license

2

Resurgence of State Rights (Dual Federalism, 1835 to 1930s)

Nullification

States have the right to nullify a federal law that in the states opinion violated the Constitution

Supreme court ruling in 1857: Congress has exceeded its powers when it abolished slavery in some of its territories. "Blacks are a subordinate and inferior class of beings" and had no right to sue in court

<u>These tendencies and developments will lead to the Civil War. Defeat of Confederacy establishes that a state cannot secede.</u>

Important

<u>The end of the Civil War brings to the so-called "Civil War Amendments":</u>

1865, 13th A.: Abolishing slavery
    1868, 14th A.: Equal protection of the laws in any state
    1870, 15th A.: Right to vote cannot bé denied by color or race

3

<u>New Deal (after 1930)</u>

Interpretation of the commerce clause ('interstate versus intrastate') in the Constitution. Results in a doctrine, holding the national government supreme in its sphere and states equally supreme in theirs

President Roosevelt expanded the power of the national government, like the National Industrial Recovery Act (1933). He was struck down by Supreme Court

Roosevelt wanted first to enlarge Supreme Court to 12 judges to weaken the "Dual Federalists". Power shifted then and new judges were elected. This leads again to Cooperative Federalism

4
New Federalism (after 1969 with President Nixon and Reagan)

Devolution process, intending to pass many federal functions on to states. Since 1994 a renewed effort by Republicans in the Congress to shift important functions back to the states. First key issue was welfare

Block Grants = funds from national government for some general policy area with the flexibility for states to decide where to spend it

<u>Available Grants:</u>

Operational grants (like running state child-care programs)

Capital grants (like building local wastewater treatment plants)

Entitlement grants (like transferring income to families)

New form of control tells the state what it must do, period, the "mandates"

Most mandates concern civil rights and environmental protection like 'Americans with Disabilities Act' or 'Water Quality Act'

5

<u>Federalism in 21st century</u>

Hot issues related to federalism for example marijuana, same sex marriage, health care reform, abortion

Chapter 3

Civil Liberties and Civil Rights

~

YOU NEED TO KNOW

- **The US system has a fundamental commitment to the rule of law. The Constitution defines the action of the government and hold's it accountable**
- **The actual scope and implementation of our civil liberties is determined by the Supreme Court Rulings and its changes**
- **The Supreme Court incorporated most of the guarantees in the Bill of Rights. The court also limits states in their activities and enforces federal standards**
- **The Protection of civil liberties is the hallmark of American government**

- **After 9/11 there is more a struggle visible of how to balance security and authority and civil liberties and civil rights**

Civil Liberties

The basic freedoms that citizens enjoy from governmental interference, such as the freedoms of speech, press, assembly, and religion. The guarantees of due process and other specific protections accorded to criminal defendants

The Bill of Rights spells out the Civil Liberties

Civil Rights

They are based on the 14th Amendment (equal protection clause). The civil rights refer to freedom from governmental discrimination (for ex. unequal treatment) based on some individual characteristic such as race, gender, or disability

Bill of Rights – First Ten Amendments of the Constitution

The Bill of Rights only applies to the federal government. The states had to incorporate these rights into their constitution. The 14th Amendment speaks about incorporating these rights as state requirement

<u>Due process clauses</u>

These Clauses in the 5th and 14th Amendment prevent the federal government from depriving people of life, liberty, or property without fair proceedings

<u>Substantive due process</u>

A judicially created concept whereby the due process clauses of the 5th and 14th Amendment can be used to strike down laws, deemed to be unfair

The Supreme Court has reaffirmed that the Bill of Rights does not limit state rights

Although the Bill of Rights stands equal to the Constitution, the implementation of Civil Liberties is often hindered by the states

<u>*Talking Point:*</u>
Does enumerating specific rights lead to the omission of other?

<u>Not Absolute Rights</u>

The Bill of Rights are not absolute rights. This means for example that the first Amendment of free speech is regulated by the concept of libel and slander

The same goes for the second amendment, "the right to bear arms". It is not an absolute right and can be regulated

First Amendment: Freedoms of Speech, Press and Assembly

First Amendment rights are essential to democratic process (but not incorporated in all states until the 20th century)
　　Supreme Court distinguishes between actions that are constitutional and not

<u>Freedom of Speech</u>

Not very clear defined
　　It is not an absolute right
　　Restriction with 'Espionage Act of 1917' in a situation of 'clear and present danger'
　　Schenck versus USA: leaflets to prevent military draft. Ruling that every act depends on the circumstances
　　"Bad Tendency Test", rights can be taken away if the situation requires it

<u>Talking Points:</u>
　　"How and where to draw the line?"
　　How can obscenity be tested and is it part of the first Amendment?

<u>Libel and Slander</u>

First amendment does not protect libel (written defamation of character) nor slander (spoken defamation of character)

The Supreme Court has set though high standards:
　　Stromberg versus CA: A red flag can be flown in a youth camp
　　Texas versus Johnson: US flag can be burned

False Advertisement

The 1st Amendment does not protect commercial advertisement. The government can though require warning labels be printed on products such as tobacco, alcohol and drugs

Freedom of Press

Important is the principle of "no prior restraint", not allowing any censorship before publication

Important rulings of the Supreme Court to cement this right:
　　Near versus Minnesota

A case that established the "no prior restraint" clause. In this case, the Saturday Press cannot be controlled prior to publishing

NY Times versus United States

The NY Times can publish the so called 'Pentagon Papers', that were classified papers related to the Vietnam war

Freedom of Assembly

The freedom to peaceably assembly is guaranteed by the 1st amendment, but it is not absolute. They are certain restriction placed on this right in regard of <u>time, place and manner</u>
Basically, it means, that people can assembly anytime and anywhere, but need to observe certain public restrictions

First Amendment: Freedom of Religion

The First Amendment contains two religion clauses (establishment and exercise clause) and they have caused much controversy

<u>Establishment Clause</u>
The establishment clause prevents government from imposing religion on citizens and it is the basis of the separation between church and state
It prohibits the government from supporting financially any religion

<u>"Lemon test" (established 1971) = created to test if a law violates the establishment clause:</u>

Laws must have a secular purpose
    Their primary effect is neither to advance nor inhibit religion
    They do not lead to excessive government entanglement with religion

Talking Point:

Discuss the battle between 'prayers in school' and displaying religious symbols on public property. Example: Removing of a granite monument to the Ten Commandments in the Alabama judicial building in 2001

Free Exercise Clause

This provision protects the right of citizens to practice their religion
    But deciding what is permissible and what constitutes a religion has led to many controversies:
    Jehovah's witnesses were arrested during World War II for not saluting the flag and not serving in the military
    In general, the Supreme Court has made clear the distinction between <u>religious belief (protected</u>) and <u>religious action (not protected</u>)

The Right of Privacy

This right of privacy is comprised from:

- 1st Amendment (assembly implies privacy)
- 3rd Amendment (quartering soldiers)
- 4th Amendment (unreasonable searches)
- 5th Amendment (self-incrimination)
- 9th Amendment (a right not enumerated does not mean the right does not exist)
- 14th Amendment (fundamental rights to be incorporated)

Natural Rights Tradition

The Declaration of Independence entitles human beings to their natural rights

The Supreme Court recognizes rights of privacy that are not enumerated, like in the rulings on abortion, homosexual rights, and the right to die

Abortions

The Supreme Court strikes down a law in Connecticut to make it a crime to use birth control (1965)

Roe v. Wade (1973): Texas law criminalized abortions. The court says this is not constitutional. Conflict between the privacy right of a woman to control her own body versus the state's interest in protecting the life of a fetus

In June 2022, the U.S. Supreme Court overturned *Roe v. Wade*, opening the door for states to ban abortion outright. In the year since the decision, 14 states have made abortion illegal

The Rights of LGBTs

Bowers versus Hardwick (1986):

Georgia made it a felony by up to 20 years in prison to engage in oral or anal sex (also for heterosexual couples). The Supreme Court upheld the law

In 2003 this verdict was overturned, arguing that laws criminalizing private, consensual homosexual conduct have no rational basis

The Supreme Court allowed homosexual marriages in June 2015

The Right to Die

The Supreme Courts defines that patients have the constitutional right to refuse medical treatment, but this right must be balanced against the competing interests of states

It ruled that privacy right does not include the right to commit suicide

The Rights of Criminal Defendants

Some provisions of the Bill of Rights protect against "double jeopardy" and self-incrimination

But the due process clauses of the 5th and 14th Amendment require states and federal government to follow fair procedure before taking away a person's life or liberty

Concept of procedural due process = must follow proceedings before taking away a person's life, liberty or property

Constitution and Amendments Criminal to protect Defendant Rights

provides for the 'writ of habeas corpus' (releasing prisoner who is being detained illegally

prohibits 'bills of attainder' (laws against someone being punished without a trial)

'ex post facto' laws (to make an action illegal retroactively)

The 5th Amendment gives the right to grand jury indictment

The 6th Amendment requires trial by jury in criminal cases

federal: 12 people; states: more than 6 jurors

The 6th Amendment requests legal representations for those who cannot afford it

The 8th Amendment protects against excessive bail

The 8th Amendment bans "cruel and unusual punishment"

"Miranda" warning since 1966

In addition to reading the rights to somebody under arrest, it also gives exclusionary rule: preventing illegally seized evidence from being introduced in criminal trials

The Death Penalty

34 states still administer the death penalty
From 1976 to 2012 were 478 inmates executed in Texas. In California, only 13 human beings

Terrorism and Civil Liberties

After 9/11 the pendulum between protecting civil liberties and combating terrorism was in strong favor of the latter. In October 2001, Congress passed he USA Patriot Act to expand government power

Examples and Controversies:

US-citizens with Japanese decent were put into camps in WWII
Warrantless wiretaps by NSA
Administration claimed the right to detain terror suspects, including US citizens, indefinitely without charge and without access to a lawyer. Supreme Court limited this provision by upholding the constitutional right for US citizens to consult a lawyer and contest their detention before an independent tribunal
Supreme Court rules in 2006: Military commissions were not authorized by congress and violate international law

Civil Rights

Slavery and the Constitution

Several sections of the Constitution sanctioned the practice of slavery

Art.1, Sec.9 says not to abolish slave trade until 1808

Art.4, Sec.2 contains the 'fugitive slave clause', being legally bound to return a fugitive slave if they escaped to another state

Constitution did nothing to protect slaves. It left it up to the states to decide on slavery. Missouri compromise in 1820 says no slavery north of 36 degrees' latitude line; this compromise was later banned by the Supreme Court

Slavery and the Supreme Court

The so called "Amistad" case, was a victory against slavery, by allowing slaves who did revolt against the captain and ending up in the US to return to Sierra Leone

Scott v. Sandford case does not allow a slave to sue in federal court

Supreme Court upheld slavery in the beginning of its existence, but changed marginally position until the Civil War. After the war a new era for former slaves in theory, but the praxis was far from the truth

After Civil War and the ratification of Amendments 13th, 14th and 15th, the so called 'civil war amendments', the Southern States passed laws known as "Black Codes". These laws were introduced to perpetuate discrimination

Black Codes

Congress does not have authority to outlaw private discrimination
Louisiana requires for a freed person to have a home within 20 days or be arrested and hired out for the rest of the year
Many more state laws about prohibition of taking certain professions, living quarters, marrying whites and so on

Civil Rights Act of 1875

outlawed discrimination in businesses such as restaurants, hotels, theaters

Ruling Plessy versus Fergusan in 1896

This Supreme Court ruling established the 'separate but equal doctrine'. The Supreme Court upholds a Louisiana law that prohibits blacks to sit in a white railroad car. Argument that this procedure is in line with the 14th Amendment (equal protection of the law)

Jim Crow Laws

The Supreme Court rulings lead to the proliferation of state and local laws requiring the segregation of races (segregated schools, no interracial marriage, prohibition)

No voting for Blacks

Blacks must pay <u>Poll Taxes</u> to vote

<u>Literacy Tests</u>: more than just read and write, but specific questions (suspended in the Voting Rights Act from 1965)

Grandfather clauses: allows illiterate Whites to vote if they can prove that their grandfather voted before Civil War (struck down in 1915)

African American Rights in the 20th Century

1909 Founding of the NAACP (National Ass. For the Advancement of Colored People)

fighting for equal rights with court challenges

<u>Brown v. Board of Education (1954)</u>

The Supreme Court overturns the 'separate but equal' doctrine and declared racially segregated schools for unconstitutional

This leads to School desegregation, but is slowed down by the South (only 2% of black school children are integrated in 1964)

1957 National guard in Arkansas blocks entry of Blacks in High School. President Eisenhower federalizes the National Guard and turns the blockade into support

Civil Rights Act of 1965

It contains six major provisions

- **It barred arbitrary discrimination in voter registration**
- **It outlawed discrimination in public accommodations associated with interstate commerce, such as hotels and restaurants**
- **It authorized the U.S. Justice Department to file lawsuits o forces the desegregation of public schools**
- **It authorized federal funds to be withheld from programs if discrimination is present**
- **It banned discrimination in employment based on race, color, religion, national origin or sex. It created the Equal Employment Opportunities Commission to enforce the ban**
- **It expanded the power of the U.S. Commission on Civil Rights, a watchdog group investigating abuses and recommending remedies**

<u>Civil Rights Movement</u>

Dr. Martin Luther King Jr. as the most prominent figure

Congress of Racial Equality (CORE): Freedom riders in busses

Outcry about the police brutality helps Congress to act: Civil Rights Act of 1964

March on Montgomery helps to implement changes, like Voting Rights Act of 1965, outlaws' literacy tests and provides federal oversight of elections

<u>Woman and Equal Rights</u>

Women gain right to vote in 1920 (19th Amendment)
    Equal protection clause.
    Women's Rights in the workplace (no women allowed in Princeton/Yale until 1969)
    Equal Rights Amendment for Woman: never ratified, only 35 states ratified it, but 38 states are necessary

<u>LGBT rights</u>

1986 Supreme Court upheld the right of states to criminalize private, consensual gay sex. Now same sex marriages are legal
    In 2011 President Obama and British Premier Cameron challenge countries that go against gay rights, like Nigeria
    These two examples show changes and development in public opinion and its implication for the "rule of the land"

Chapter 4

Public Opinion

~

D<u>oes Pubic Opinion make a difference?</u>

Public Opinion Definition = overall opinion of citizens on political issues

Some people though, have stronger voices and therefore a greater impact

Public Opinion is measured by opinion polls and weighted equally

If public opinion enters political decision making is not the simple sum of everyone's opinion on an issue

James Madison argued for a strong role of public opinion, because the social and intellectual elites do not have the monopoly on truth

<u>Political Culture</u>

Public opinion is in part a product of a country's political culture. Political Culture changes slowly

Alexis de Toqueville, a perceptive French observer of American Politics, noticed this in the 1830s in his book <u>"Democracy in America"</u>:

"America has emphasis on individuality and freedom, reliance on local politics and voluntary organizations, restlessness and desire for progress."

American Public Aspects

<u>Political Tolerance</u>

The American overall level of tolerance for dissent is low, but improving

<u>Example:</u>

In 1954 88% of Americans thought that someone opposed to religion should not teach in college

<u>Trust in Government</u>

Requirement in Democracy is the healthy skepticism about individual officeholders

Trust in government has fluctuate widely over the last decades

Talking Point:

Trust in government has dropped overall since the 1950s.
Compare Americans to other countries and define reasons

Political Efficacy

Efficacy = belief that citizens can affect what the government does
This belief has declined over the last decades, but is still higher than in other countries

Political Knowledge

Americans love their leaders but dislike politicians
Often people do not know about key-issues, but have only one or two agendas (right to bear arms, abortion, immigration)

American Exceptionalism

Values that are thought to be American: freedom, equality, individualism
Immigrant History: 'melting pot culture'; everybody can make it
Certain common Attitude: 'nation building', 'policeman of the world', "best country"

<u>Talking Point:</u>

Does an American exceptionalism exist? And if so, how do you define it

Political Socialization

Political Socialization describes the process, how people learn values

Various sources of learning are called 'agents of political socialization'

People also learn political identities

Families: parents have credibility

Peer Groups: friends and other social contacts have credibility

Schools: government tries to reshape a country's political culture

College: strong formative influence (students become independent)

Media: source of political information and filter of what is important

Political events: can be life changing, like Great Depression, Vietnam War, 9/11

<u>Group Identities</u>

<u>Age</u>

An aging population affects politics. Older people get more influential and influence political decision.

Examples:
   Social Security
   Medicaid
   Legislation

Race and Ethnic Groups

America is diverse racially and ethnically
   African Americans have in general a lower income and are pro Democrats
   Hispanics are passionate about immigration. They are normally conservative, but appalled by republican approach
   Asian Americans have special values like education and strong family business ties

Religion

Americans are very religious (for almost 60% God is important). Religion is an important determinant of voting behavior
   Catholics tend to be Democrats, but with abortion and gay marriage change in political behavior
   Protestants are equally divided between parties
   Jews have more a tendency of being liberal on economic and social issues

Muslims identify with Democrats through experiences with 'War on Terror'

Social Class

Large income differences. The word "class" does not exist in the U.S.A., but this is more a traditional thought than a fact

The rich favor Republicans and the poor Democrats. This distinction gets more blurred during the Trump presidency. Underprivileged people vote for Trump and Republicans

Gender

Women vote in greater numbers for Democrats

Regions of the USA

"Red" states: South and Mountain States
"Blue" states: West Coast and North East States

Public Opinion changes

The changing in public opinion and overall attitudes is caused by the replacement of older people with younger people. The shift is slow and gradually, but if the turning point is reached, nothing stops the change

Changes in Party Identification

Party identification changes slowly. Recently the numbers of Independents have increased dramatically (over 40% in 2008) are independents

Talking Point:

In which areas has public opinion changed in the last decade?

Public Opinion is measured

Poll

A poll is a set of questions asked of a carefully constructed sampling of a population. Sample is likely to mirror the total population

Best way to achieve this is a random sample

Random Sample

drawn from the full population in such a way that every member of the population has an equal probability of belonging to the sample

Margin of Error

Statistical measure of how much the sample estimate from a poll is likely to deviate from the true amount in the full population

Different Forms of Polls

Cluster Sampling: random selection of different locations
    Random digit Dialing: telephone numbers are dialed randomly
    Internet Polling: Americans agree to fill out a survey

Polls in Political Campaigns

Tracking Polls: short, simple polls on one issue
    Exit Polls: At the exit of a voting station at Election Day
    Push Polls: Questions to present negative information about an opposing candidate

Limitation of Polls and Questions

How are the questions phrased?
    Artificial situation in answering questions

How large is the sample?

Way of contacting the people decides who it is (telephone, internet)

Political Culture – America in the World

Political System copied by many states in Latin America. Similar institutions with federalism, elected president, a bicameral legislature, and the separation of powers

Interesting fact, that although the institutions were developed similar, it did not produce a political system capable of both effective government and the protection of liberty

It seems, that Americans have specific 'moral and intellectual characteristics', that made the system work

Political Culture

Definition of <u>political culture</u> = Distinctive and patterned way of thinking about how political and economic life ought to be carried out

Important Aspect:

In America, everybody is equal politically, but it is not important to have economic equality. But normally economic wealth comes with political influence and power

Important American Elements

<u>Liberty:</u> preoccupation with rights. Freedom to do whatever is legal

    <u>Equality:</u> equal vote and equal chance to participate

    <u>Democracy:</u> officials should be accountable

    <u>Civic duty:</u> people ought to take community affairs seriously

    <u>Individual responsibility:</u> individuals are responsible for their own actions and well-being

    House of Representative initiated a committee to find "Un-American Activities"

Metric System

Officially, the United States is one of only three countries (Liberia and Burma being the other two) that has not officially switched to the metric system. The US uses the "customary system" which is also known as the "English" or "Imperial" system, because it has its roots in the UK

Money Color

For a long time, American currency was known for only appearing in one color- green. Most other countries color-code different denominations, or simply use money that features multiple colors on individual bills. The greenness of American money has its roots in the 19th Century. At the time, green dye was rare, and thus considered difficult for counterfeiters to obtain. This bit of American uniqueness is now slowly being phased out, as new US bills being introduced with multi-colored inks

Official Language

Though most Americans speak English as their sole language, the American government in its long history has never bothered to make English the official language of the country. Almost all countries in the world have at least one official language, which in turn serves as the language the government is mandated to provide services to its citizens in. In the US, by contrast, the federal government will provide various services in dozens of different languages, should they be requested

The only other countries without an official language are the UK, Australia, and Sweden

Treaties

As many internationalists in both the US and elsewhere never tire of pointing out, the government of the United States often takes radically un-mainstream positions when it comes to ratifying international treaties

The Convention on the Rights of the Child

The United States is one of 10 countries that has not ratified the Convention on the Elimination of All Forms of Discrimination Against Women (US the only western nation)

Exit from the Paris Climate Agreement by the Trump administration - rejoined in 2020

Not ratifying Trade Agreements, although partners agreed,

like Trans-Pacific Partnership (TPP) and The Transatlantic Trade and Investment Partnership (T-TIP)

The Capital District

In most countries, the capital city is just that — a city that also happens to be the capital. But in the United States the situation is a bit weirder. The city of Washington is not part of any state in the union, rather it is the only city in a specially-created "District of Columbia," which is a unique political entity unto itself. The logic was that this was supposed to give the capital a sort of neutral status, because it would not "belong" to any one state

Nowadays a lot of people question this concept, however. The half-million residents of Washington, for example, largely get screwed by the deal. Since they do not legally live in any state they do not get to elect any members of Congress (instead they get to elect one hack "delegate" who has no voting powers, and can only watch). They still get taxed and governed by the federal government though, which has prompted them to bring back "no taxation without representation!" as a rebellious rallying cry

The Economic System

Liberty is important in the US economy. The ability to create a corporation and to operate a business is much easier in America. Less administrative hurdles

Free-enterprise economic system in comparison to European social capitalism

Americans tolerate economic inequality, but not political

inequality

Civic Role of Religion

Puritanism and Catholicism. Both religions promote very strong family values and support a hard, but proud working life

There are many different branches of the Protestant church and many more different groups who follow specific preaching's in the bible. Strong influence especially in the Midwest and the South

America in the World

The main goals of American foreign policy are security, prosperity, and improving the world

Security

Defense budget (2014) = $600 Billion (1/3 of the worlds budget and 10times more than China). This economical and therefore technological dominance has been maintained so far

In the 18th and 19th centuries, the US believed that its security is based on its geographic isolation. Strong tendencies to today's policies

1823: President James Monroe created his 'Monroe Doctrine', isolating America from the world

20th century: Advances in technology make distances

disappear. The economic interdependence makes it necessary for America to be part of the world

After WWII security policy known as <u>deterrence</u> (discouraging attacks with military strength). The Policy always has swung between preventive war or appeasement

New security treats through terrorist groups. Before foreign Policy was defined as 'resistance to Fascism and Communism. 9/11/2001 changed this radically

Expanding definition of self-defense, from a narrow concept of continental self-defense to an expansive, global vision with very broad limits

Economic

World Trade Organization (WTO) 1995 = most important international organization for promoting trade

North American Free Trade Agreement (NAFTA)

1990s End of Cold War – Americans unsure of their place in the world

New politics in the era of President Trump = going back to Isolationism and ending multinational agreements

Many decisions of the Trump administration reversed by the Biden Administration. Rejoining International Organizations:

- United Nations Educational, Scientific and Cultural Organization (UNESCO)
- World Health Organization (WHO)
- United Nations Human Rights Council (UNHRC)
- Paris Agreement

Talking Point:
Discuss US-Membership in NATO

Foreign Policy Players

The President leads the Foreign Policy (often not prepared to understand international relations and the complexity of topics)
Foreign policy actors are Secretaries of Defense and State Department. The Joint Chiefs of Staff (JCOS) and the Director of the CIA. In the era of Trump, the involvement of the different actors has change significant
Important: National Security Council and Department of Homeland Security (DHS)

Congress

needs to approve treaties
power to declare war and provide for common defense
regulates foreign commerce
Funding for foreign and military initiatives
Senate needs to confirm president's nomination for cabinet members and high-ranking officials (CIA director)

Talking Points:
How has American political culture changed over the past 100 years? Discuss mistrust of government and tension between traditional moral issues and personal freedom

Chapter 5

Democracy

~

YOU NEED TO KNOW

- **Understand the different forms of Democracy**
- **Explain the difference between Politics, Government and Citizenship**
- **Know the Four Basic Values in American Politics**
- **Define the Primary Political Ideologies**

Different Forms of Democracy

How does the United States compare to other democracies? Understand that important measures of a democratic society are the rights of Citizens and the ability and restriction of the government to interfere in people's daily life

The word 'democracy' comes from the Greek. It means "Rule by the people" (demos = people + cracy = to rule)

Understand that the first form of democracy was derived and practiced in Ancient Greece, especially in Athens. All citizens (free men with property) could vote

<u>Talking Point:</u>

Discuss social democracies, like the Scandinavian countries, that interfere in Health Care, Child Care and other social aspects of their citizens

Direct Democracy

This is the closest approach to the concept of "rule by the people". In a direct democracy citizens come together to discuss and vote on an issue. This form of democracy still exists partly in Switzerland. Direct Democracy works in small communities with specific issues

Talking Point:

Direct democracy is assumed to only work for simple issues. This brings up the question of elites and the general discussion if uneducated people should be able to vote

Indirect Democracy

In the United States a direct democracy is impossible. Almost all democracies today are indirect democracies also called **representative democracies**

All eligible citizens can vote to choose from alternative candidates. These candidates – after being elected – are the people in charge of making laws and decisions. This election process starts on the local level with majors and supervisors; continues at the state level with governors and state legislators; and summits on the federal level with presidents and members of congress

Concept of Citizen, a fully qualified and legally recognized member of a country

Interesting to note, that former felons who have completed their prison sentences are still not allowed to vote in certain states. They need to petition to be reinstated

Government and Politics

Politics is the process by which collective decisions are made. These decisions are binding for everyone in the country

Collective decisions are for example laws, system of taxes, budget spending, employment

The process of politics includes not only the government and its representatives, but also the public opinion, the media and interest groups

The government in every country makes the decision in the end. It functions to keep internal order, to develop infrastructure and to interact with other governments

The government also has the legal right to use force to ensure that laws are followed

What makes an Indirect Democracy work?

Certain requirements are necessary to make a democracy work. They are four major aspects:

1

<u>Free election with real choice</u>

All political contestants with their party, group or affiliation have the right to participate in the election. Ample space is to be given to these political alternatives in the media to reflect the possible choices

2

Broad participation in the elections

A democracy only works with active participants who understand that the right to vote is very essential to their role as citizen. A low participation in the election shows voter boredom, disinterest and a lack of civic understanding

In return a government must ensure that voters can vote and that there are enough polls without distinction of neighborhoods

3

Freedom of speech and media

A basic requirement of democracy is sufficient individual freedom and open debate. Freedom of Speech and Freedom of Press are mandatory for any democratic society

4

Right to organize

Citizens need to have the right to organize themselves freely. This includes political parties, organizations and interest groups to focus and pool their agenda. The right for free movement and free assembly is a very part of this

Challenges of Democracy

Democracy has its imperfection and yet it is the only form of government that implies all people are of equal worth and have the right to be heard

<u>A democracy has an in-transient dilemma:</u>
<u>The need to ensure majority rule and protecting minority rights</u>

A majority is 50% plus 1 and it allows an official to be voted in. The majority prevails obviously, and yet the government must protect the right of the minority. May it be racial, ethnical, religious or any other factor, everybody needs to be heard and respected

Democracy versus Republic

Sometimes these two concepts are confused. A republic is just a country not ruled by a monarch. As we have seen in chapter 2, the Founders of the United States used the term 'republic' to make clear that the elected representatives would govern on basis of their own understanding

This is a strong proof in the founder's belief that not God or divine intuition gives the new leaders a guidance, but their own understanding and experience

Functions of Government

Government needs to provide services for its citizens. To do so, it interferes with the lives of people, an ambivalence that is often perceived by citizens as overreaching and being ruled. And yet, the United States government provides fewer goods and services than most other wealthy countries

Talking Point:

Discuss "State of Jefferson" as an idea to create a leaner government.

They are three major functions of government

1

Maintaining Order and Safety

The government is the sole entity to use force and coercion against crimes. It also guarantees financial transactions and contracts to ensure private property

2

Providing Public Goods

Public goods include national defense, medical research, public health, public transportation. These are goods that cannot be given only to a few while withholding from others. There is an aspect of "free riders", people who take advantage of the system without contributing to it

3

Promoting General Welfare

- Infrastructure: for example, education, highways, parks
- Regulating economy to ensure it operates fairly
- Providing support for people in vulnerable positions
- Redistributing income through the federal income system and social security
- Regulating people's behavior and police to enforce it

American Values

American Values can be characterized by a strong individual self-reliance and sense of freedom. Fairness based on contribution and the belief in the rule of law. In addition, there is a relatively strong religious faith that influences the role of marriage, family, and community life

Fairness

The idea of the "American Dream" has its roots here. You get what you deserve, if you work hard you will be rewarded. A universal value in societies who allow vertical social success.

Individualism - Freedom

Individualism and the freedom to express oneself are important American values. It reflects the ability to rely on oneself and make decisions. Americans are rather subject to as little as possible governmental control

Religion

In comparison to other developed nation, many more Americans declare themselves as religious. Many values are rooted here. America has been a pioneer in many aspects of social life (same-sex-marriage, abortion) and at the same time home of many extreme religious belief systems

The Rule of Law

There is a clear determination that laws govern the land. It embodies the concept that people must be treated fairly and that the government is to be restricted and guided by the law to do the same. The Bill of Rights, the first ten Addendums to the Constitution guarantee these freedoms and rights to all Americans

American Ideologies

<u>Ideology = interconnected set of ideas that form our idea of politics</u>

There are two main ideologies in America, Conservatism and Liberalism. Due to the strong value of individualism and freedom other political ideas have never become mainstream

<u>Conservatism</u>

A fundamental idea within Conservatism is the right for government intervention on behalf of moral views, like family and schools. But it denies government involvement in the economic realm, relying on market powers

<u>Liberalism</u>

Within the liberal movement, governmental intervention is welcomed to reduce economic inequality. Opposite to conservatism, it denies the government any interference in religious or social views

There are some minor ideological views represented in US politics, that just need to be mentioned:

Libertarian

Maximum individual freedom with little government intervention

Socialism

Major industries cannot be in the hands of powerful individuals, but need to be regulated by the state to ensure a just social interaction between "capital" and "work"

Fascism

A nationalist, racist ideology that lead to the catastrophe of the Nazi regime in Germany and the Second World War. Elements of this autocratic ideas have been recently flourishing more in the US due to immigration concerns for the economically lower end of the population

Chapter 6

Political Parties

~

YOU NEED TO KNOW

- **Political Parties are the lubricant that allows democracy to flow smoothly"**
- **American Political Parties are the oldest in the world**
- **Historically to be Republican or Democrat was a serious commitment**
- **Today parties are weak due to rules and regulations.**
- **Sense of commitment is lost**
- **Federal system of government also produced a decentralized party system**

Definition "Political Party"

"**A** *political party is a group that seeks to elect candidates to public office by supplying them with a label – 'a party identification' – by which they are known to the electorate.*"

<u>Other Aspects</u>

Periods of strong support of party candidates with money and supporters, followed by weak periods of disinterest
In the USA party affiliation is printed on ballot – in Australia and Israel for example, party affiliation does not appear on ballot

<u>Three areas to measure strength of a political party</u>
<u>(within these parameters, the US-parties are weak)</u>:

Label in minds of voters
Organization that recruits and campaigns for candidates
Set of leaders who try to control different branches of.
government

<u>*Talking Point:*</u>
Discuss why American Parties are weak in comparison to other countries

The Two-Party System

U.S.A. has a two-party system. In other countries, normally more than two parties. Effects are visible in vote patterns and there is no need for coalition building

Between 1888 and 2000 Republicans won 17 presidential elections, Democrats won 15 elections. It shows a balanced power between parties

Historically Democrats strong in South, Republicans strong in North East. This regional divide has changed and is reversed now (New Deal and Civil Rights movement changed affiliation)

The US has a Plurality System, meaning: "Winner takes it all"

Different systems in Europe. European Countries elections are based on proportional representation. This means a party submits a list of candidates for parliament and gets members elected in relation to total votes (5% clause in Germany to be able to be counted for seats in parliament)

France requests members of parliament to be elected with absolute majority

Two party system stabilizes democracy. Only times of bitter dissent create ideologies and makes it difficult to find a compromise

Comparison to Europe

Candidates for elective office are nominated by party leaders

Campaigns is run by the party with party funds and workers

Once in office, the elected official is expected to vote with other party members

Strong influence of party in many aspects of life (unions, schools, clubs, youth organizations etc.)

No primaries (leaders put names on ballot)

<u>Reason for this Difference</u>

Decentralized party organization and strong influence and power in states and local areas

Parties closely regulated by state and federal laws

Party leaders do not select people to run for office (chosen by voters in primary elections)

Difference between American system of separation between Congress and Presidency, the European Parliamentary system chooses the chief executive by the majority of the legislative branch

In America one does not join a party with party book, there is no real national organization

Parties are separate from other aspects of life, play only a segmental role in social context

History of Political Parties

<u>Four broad periods of party history</u>

- Creation between Founding and 1820s (First Party System)
- Two-party system emerging (President Jackson to Civil War)
- Developing comprehensive organizational form and appeal (Civil War to 1930s)
- Party reforms altering the party system (1900s, especially since New Deal)

Founding

George Washington condemns parties amidst quarreling between Hamilton and Jefferson

Parties could only develop by understanding that quarrels about issues do not undermine constitution in general

Federalists (Hamilton) versus Republicans (Jefferson)

Loose organization, stronghold Federalists in New England, Republicans in the South. The parties do not represent clear homogeneous interests

The Jacksonians

Political participation gets stronger – number of voters much higher (1824: 365k; 1840: 2 million)

Democratic party (Jacksonian) built party system from bottom to top. Start of party conventions

Two-party system emerges (Democrats and Whigs)

Republicans, founded from the Whigs around 1860, (strong in the North, Democrats strong in the South)

Era of Reform

Progressives try to change parties' structure by favoring primary elections
　　No alliances between businesses and parties
　　Introducing referendums, use of mass media

Party Realignments

Theory of critical or realigning periods
　　Realignments have occurred a few times in history caused by social issues (slavery) or economic issues (depression)
　　Party is so badly defeated that it disappears and new party emerges
　　Voters shift support from one party to another

Party Decline

Decline in party affiliation.
　　Split Ticket voting opposed to straight ticket (voters split between presidential vote and vote for Congress)
　　Office-bloc ballot versus party-column ballot = office ballot lists all candidates by office and not by party

The National Party Structure Today

No real structure on a national level, no national board
Kind of independent organizations exist on local and state level
National convention nominates the presidential candidate
Between conventions a national committee is managing party affaires
Congressional campaign committee: helps members of Congress to run for reelection
National chairman: full time position of running party day-to-day

National Conventions

Important question is the selection of delegates. It is done through a complex formula
Democrats give extra delegates to large states, Republicans to loyal states
Selection process (different commissions trying to define rules: equal division between sexes – minorities in relation to presence in state's electorate – 75% chosen at the level of congressional district or lower)
Restrictions of party leaders and elected officials have been changed to benefit the establishment. Therefore, majority on 'super-delegates' (elected office holders)

State and local Parties

Organized under state law

strong party bosses or elected officials handpick people to run for office

More and more public figures ('name recognition') with money come into the races for office

The Political Machine

Definition

"A political machine is a party organization that recruits its members using tangible incentives, like money, political jobs, favors. It is characterized by a high degree of leadership control over member activity."

Especially important in the 18th and 19th century when immigrants were recruited for party work and given jobs in local or federal bureaucracy

Abuses of the machine with kickbacks and favors. Generating money to employ party members in jobs and functions

System has changed due to education, income and sophistication weakening the power of party officials

Ideological Parties

They were always parties of the very edge of the political system active in America. These parties were mostly ideological and high principled

Examples of parties that are still exist today: Socialist Workers Party, Socialist Labor Party, Libertarian, Green Party

Nominating a President

A winning candidate was thought of someone who can compromise. The last election showed, that polarization is a new method to win the vote

Primaries (general voters) versus Caucus (only party followers)

States have primaries, caucuses or a combination of both

Normally only passionate voters are voting in the primaries. Therefore, tendencies of more left- or right leaning support

Changing incentives of being a delegate: 1980 only 14% of democratic senators were delegates, in 1956 90% of senators were delegates

Conventions are orchestrated Show events. The nominee has been decided by the votes

Chapter 7

Nominations and Elections

~

Concept

"**E**lections are meant to ensure one of the fundamental qualities of our democracy: a government responsive to the people's wishes"

Development of Elections in America

The current system of elections in the US underwent a lengthy evolution before becoming the complicated system of today

Voting started out as a right given only to a few and no is a right for every citizen above the age of 18

Felons cannot vote and in 12 states they can never vote again

Talking Points:

Can this right to vote be allowed as an absolute? The Framers had a restrictive, more elite view of the voting rights

Strong influence on voter decision with 'fake news', 'rumors', or the direct influence of foreign powers to create confusion

Historically

Only House of Representative was directly elected

Only citizen with required property laws could vote

Changes

Former male slaves voting rights, 1870

Senate directly elected, 1913

Women voting rights, 1920

Voting age 18 years, 1971

Voting Rights Act of 1965

Gives the Attorney General the authority to bar discrimination in voting rights by race

New procedures for voting

The government, not the political parties, now prints the official ballots

Ballots include the names of candidates from all parties

Ballots are distributed only at polling places

Ballots are cast secretly, not openly

Elections as Tools for Accountability

Elections make officials accountable to citizens
Accountability = capacity to impose consequences on officials
for their actions

Three Types of Elections

Primary elections (nominees from a party and independents
appear on the ballot, to be chosen to compete in the general
election)
General elections (all the voters make final choice)
Recall elections (offered through State law statues)

Complex Elections

In America, many officials are elected by voting
Especially on the local level there is an era of different
positions that are gained through voting, like Supervisors, Sheriffs,
Councilmen- and women

The Presidential Campaign

It starts with the nomination, which is contested state by state in primary elections or caucuses

First states are most important, like Iowa and New Hampshire

Difference between caucuses (IA, MN, NV for example select convention delegates) and primary elections (vote directly for candidates)

Open primaries versus closed primaries (meaning either only party affiliates or everybody)

Road to Nomination (long and tricky)

Prior fame and name recognition is important (governors, celebrities)

Media coverage is important

In the televised debates the performance is absolutely deciding

Mobilize volunteers and energize them

Money for advertising, contributions, funds

Timeline

Iowa Caucus, opens nominations; followed by South Carolina Democratic primary elections

Early contests are important to stay in the race

States are scrambling to front-load their delegate selection

Super Tuesday (18 States are voting)

Participation in Caucus and Primaries is low. Often left for activists to voice their more extreme views

Talking Points:

Do attendees represent the party spectrum?

In America, wide range of candidates to choose from. Candidate

*is not nominated by the party, but decides to run (question of
'lacking experience' and other flaws)*

National Convention

Role has changed over time; today no more questions about who
has the most delegates. Since 1972 the frontrunner is clearly
elected through primaries and caucuses

Conventions are managed affaires with entertainment and
attention grabbers

General Election

Congressional Elections

Incumbent members of Congress, the current members of
Congress, have an advantage

House members and Senators control to a certain extend
the news

Incumbent has staff to support constituents

Ability to add benefits to legislation. Easier access to campaign
contribution and experience gives current member an advantage

Voters look at party lines to win the Congress

Nomination process for congressional candidates is like that of the president. House members are nominated for each district and senators in statewide conventions

'Open seat', means a chance for somebody new

'Party Accountability', holding the party accountable at elections

Split ticket voting more popular. Dividing votes not along party lines, but along preferences

Manipulation of District Boundaries

District boundaries are sometimes manipulated to gain reelection

State governments are responsible for setting up boundaries

'Gerrymandering' – makes opponent loose votes

Turnover of incumbent officials is much lower than in other countries

Electoral Systems and their Effects

Single-member-district, plurality (SMDP) electoral system

"An electoral system in which the country is divided into districts, each of which elects a single member to the Congress or parliament

The candidate with the largest numbers of votes wins the seat. The single-member-district produces a two- party system"

Proportional Representations (PR)

"An electoral system in which seats are allocated to parties in proportion to their shares of the vote. A proportional voting system produces more parties."

Electoral College

"The system by which presidents are elected in the US. Voters vote for a set of electors, and the set that wins casts its vote for the candidate to which it is pledged."

Framers did not want a direct electoral connection between Citizens and President

Each state selects a group of electors equal to the number of members of Congress

Until 1816 electors were appointed by the states legislators. Since then many changes due to development of national parties and a stronger belief in democracy (elites)

Popular versus Electoral votes. Especially important in the 2000 elections

'Strategic campaigning', it makes sense to pay little attention to states that cannot be won

Small population versus large population states

Casting pledged votes (no legal provision to cast votes as pledged)

Discussion about changing the Electoral College and to replace with straight popular vote. Different proposals have been made, like dividing states into congressional districts like in NE and Maine. To amend the Constitution is hard to accomplish due to the amendment process and the elimination of battleground states

Presidential Election Process – From Primaries to National Election

Presidential Primaries and Caucuses

An election for President of the United States occurs every four years. Before the election, most candidates for President go through a series of state primaries and caucuses

State primaries occur through a secret ballot. There are two types of primaries: closed and open. During a closed primary, you can vote only for a candidate belonging to the same political party as you. During an open primary, you can vote for a candidate of any political party

Caucuses are meetings where members of political parties divide themselves into groups according to the candidate they support, with undecided voters forming into a group of their own. Each group then gives speeches supporting a candidate and tries to persuade others to join their group. At the end of the caucus, party organizers count the voters in each candidate's group and calculate how many delegates each candidate has won

When the primaries and caucuses are over, most political parties hold a national convention where the winning candidate receives a nomination

Electoral College

The Electoral College is the process used to elect the U.S President and Vice President. The process serves as a compromise between election of the President by a vote in Congress and election of the President by a popular vote of qualified citizens. The candidate with at least 270 electoral votes wins a presidential election

The process begins with the sections of the electors, followed by the meeting of the electors to vote for President and Vice President, and finally the counting of the electoral votes by Congress

Number of Electors

Each state's number of elector is equal to the number of its U.S. Senators plus the number of its U.S. Representatives. In 48 states, when a candidate receives the majority of votes, he or she receives all of a state's electoral votes. Two states, Maine and Nebraska, can split their electoral votes among the candidates. It is possible for a candidate to receive the majority of the popular vote but not of the electoral vote and lose a presidential election

Presidential Election Process

The election process begins with the primary elections, during which political parties each select a nominee to unite behind; the nominee in turn selects a Vice Presidential running mate. The candidates then face off in the general election, usually participating in debates and campaigns across the country to explain their views and plans to the voters

An election occurs every four years. Unlike other political elections, presidential elections use the Electoral College. The President and the Vice President are the only two nationally elected officials in the United States. To win election, a candidate must receive a majority of electoral votes, or if no candidate receives a majority, the House of Representatives and Senate choose the President and Vice President

Elections and the Representation of Women and Minorities

In the U.S.A., Minorities and Women are still much less proportionally elected to office (17% women – no mandatory representation like in other countries)

Part of SMDP system

Creating majority-minority districts to help ensure minority representation

Campaign Finance

Political campaigns are expensive in the US. In 2012 about 6 Billion USD were spent in America to 88 Million USD in the UK for national election

Efforts to limit the role of money in electoral politics. There is a stronger tendency now, to allow new sources of money into the electoral process

The Supreme Court rules that to "limit campaign money is to limit free speech"

<u>2002 Bipartisan Campaign Reform Act:</u>
Compliance and Disclosure = Report to FEC, Federal Election   Commission

<u>Limits to contribution was changed by the Supreme Court:</u>
To receive public financing, the presidential candidates must limit their spending. As well, it is required to "Stand by your Ad", making the statement mandatory "I approve this ad"

Independent Expenditures

More than 500 Committees active as advocacy groups, that can advertise on political issues and are not subject to regulation by the FEC
Independent campaign organization = Super PAC. They can raise unlimited amounts of money from corporations and organizations.

Super PACs

Flexibility
Degree of dependence to candidate
Large donors
Prolonged nomination contests

Chapter 8

Voting and Participation

~

There are in general two ways of participating in politics: Unconventional and Conventional

Conventional Participation

- Voting and helping the voting process
- Working for a candidate
- Joining an interest group
- Contributing to a campaign
- Writing a letter to a representative
- Running for office
- As the name indicates, conventional participation describes the traditional ways to be involved in politics

<u>Unconventional Participation</u>

- **Boycotts**
- **Demonstrations**
- **Sit-ins**
- **Occupying offices**

Many citizens perceive their democratic participation as too narrow and no-effective. In many non-democratic countries, unconventional participation is often the only open form of participation

<u>"Why is the Voter turnout lower in the US than in many countries?"</u>

19th and 20th century: voting for certain groups was restricted
   Although people became higher educated, they did not vote more

<u>Convenience and Motivation:</u>

Prior registration by voters. In other countries, automatic registration
   A study showed that participation would increase by 14% with automatic registration
   Election Day always on a Tuesday.

Paradox of Voting, in some states, like TX or CA, people know which party candidate will succeed, so there is no motivation to vote

Who votes?

Age

Young voters participate less in American elections than older voters
In 2010, age 18-24 old voted only 21.3%

Ethnicity

Asians, Hispanics and African Americans do not vote as much as Whites. Asian are the lowest with 30.8%

Income

The higher an individual's income, the more likely will he/she vote
Income under $20k only 30% voted

Thinking and Approach

What difference does it make who votes?

The outcome of the election no longer mirrors the overall population's interests accurately. Political officials will pay more attention to those groups who vote (older/richer versus younger/poorer)

Congressional Elections

Phenomena: "Midterm Elections" have a lower voter turnout. Often the vote is cast as protest against the presidential party

How People make Voting Decisions

Important question is to find out for whom voters vote, because after all, an election is the determining event in democratic policies

Thesis: The election system is intended to moderate the rate of change

They are 4 major factors influencing Voter Decisions

What they think of the candidates
How they view the state of the nation and economy
The candidates' party
Policy issues

Information Levels

Difficult to gather all the facts to make an intelligent choice. The decision is very much an emotional one, therefore the first factor "Candidates themselves" is very crucial (Same like shopping)

Development of voters to focus more on fundamental ideologies (like gun control, abortion etc.). In the last few elections a movement to "single issue decisions" can be observe

In general, the important stances of candidates on different policy positions are unknown (Example: Comment of presidential democratic candidate Lincoln Chafee that he did not know the facts about the "Glass/Stiegel Act" when he came into the Senate and had to vote right away)

Even on a more dramatic level the under-information is widespread. In a study in 2010 less than half of the questioned people knew which party did win the House and which one the Senate

The Candidates

<u>Studies show that voters look for two main qualities choosing a candidate:</u>

1

How well can she/he perform the job?
One reason why debates are important: shows the intelligence and information level of candidates

2

How honest?

Can his/her word be trusted? Indicators are consistency, speaking style and personal behavior

The State of Nation and Economy

If positive, reelection of sitting president and incumbent office holders

If negative, especially bad for presidential party: President is responsible therefore in Midterm Elections often a setback

Strong effects of the State of the Economy on voter decisions

Retrospective Voting = voters look back at the years an official has been in office and voting in accordance to their current situation (one aspect is also that with retrospective voting the government is held accountable)

Party Identification

Voters develop a party identification. Party identification does not change easily from election to election. It is therefore a stabilizing factor

Party Identification changes strongly in times of major events, like New Deal, Civil Rights Movement, Immigration

The older people get, the more they become connected to a party

"Split voting" more common, meaning voting is not more done along party lines

The major party identification in a state also determines where campaigns spent their money in time. Focus on the so-called "battleground states

Policy Issues

In general voters are unaware of a candidate's issue positions
    The party gives the label to the candidate
    Polls show which issues are most important to voters. Candidates will make them key issues

Who votes for whom?

Affiliation, birth, religion and social status are important for groups to identify with the candidate. Examples are President Obama and the African-American Community or George Bush and the born-again Christians
    Hispanic vote important as well. Many parts of the country have a majority of Hispanics, so only candidates from this group will get voted in

Political Campaigns and Voter's Choices

Candidates must develop a game plan that is in tune with the unique legal, political and financial realities of American politics
    It starts with hiring a campaign manager

Complex, technical tools are used to make campaigning a success

Polls = trying to be on the pulse of the voter
    Focus groups = like polls, but more specific to certain demographics
    Television ads = expensive, but effective
    Free Media = getting into the news – debates
    Social Networking = new forms to attract especially young voters

Election campaigns have two different kinds of ways to run

Position issues: opposing views on distinct policy issues.
    Valence issues: supporting topics everybody agrees upon.

Electoral Mobilization versus Changing Minds

A Campaign needs to ask if they want an electoral mobilization of their own base or change the minds of opposing voters. Where shall the focus lie?

Targeted Marketing

Databases of Republicans and Democrats, the so-called "lists"
    All data compiled to detect voting behavior

Pattern of consumption are indicators for voting
Gather as much information about potential voters

Talking Point:

"A gullible public is being sold a bill of goods by slick NY advertisers, whether the goods are automobiles or politicians". What do you think?

Flow Factors in a Campaign

The candidates normally only relate to position papers. Fact-filled speeches about complex issues are hard to find
Finding a winning coalition. Making sure that everyone is pleased without anyone hurting
A mishap in a debate can be devastating
Other factors are the perceptions about the state of the nation and the economy

Party Polarization among Party Affiliates

Parties are getting more polarized. This leads to isolation towards the other parties and often ideologically strong minded factions are holding the party hostage

Voter Suppression

Some observers say, that there is an increased element of voter suppression in the United States. It is also called a disenfranchisement of voters due to age, citizenship, or criminal record.

<u>The Right to vote</u>

The major difference between a 'permanent resident' (green card holder) and of an American citizen is the right to vote. The Constitution first only allowed white male citizens over the age of 21 to vote. Now, every American citizen over the age of 18 can vote.

Chapter 9

Interest Groups

∼

YOU NEED TO KNOW

- They are more than 200,000 associations and organizations in the US. This is partly due to the expansion of the US government since World War II
- Interest groups are playing an important role in American government; they are necessary for the political process

D<u>efinition</u>

"Interest groups are associations or organizations of individuals who share a common interest and assert their collective strength in the political process to protect – and in some cases, expand – that interest."

The aim is to influence the government's policies on all levels

This purpose distinguishes it from a political party which aims to win power by attaining an office

Many reasons for interest groups to be formed like strengthen a profession or avocation, pursuing a political or social agenda or shaping a policy debate

Talking Point:

Interest groups are 'pressure groups' and pursue their 'special interests'. How can it be allowed that one group in the society can put their aims first through power, money and influence?

History

Ambivalent attitude from the Framers: James Madison wrote: 'ability of interests to organize is the essence of freedom' and yet 'mischief of factions'

Organized lobbying by individuals and interest groups predates the Republic. During colonial times, merchants, manufacturers, religious and ethnic groups hired agents to lobby members of the British parliament for favorable legislative treatment

Similar strategies then as today: cultivating relationships, letter writing campaigns, drafting legislation, making financial contributions, forming coalitions

The Revolutionary Period

<u>Appearance of more and more public interest organizations:</u>

Bill of Rights Society = bringing suffrage (right to vote) to the colonies
    Sons of Liberty = group of laborers and tradesmen to repeal unjust laws

Constitutional Convention

Decision was made early to hold the convention in secret and locked doors to prevent influences from lobbyists
    Development and industrialization of the country makes new interest groups emerge. Trying to prevent Congress from passing laws and regulations hostile to their interests

The Rise of Interest Groups

Two major events: Civil War (1860s) and Progressive Movement 1900s to 1920s)

<u>Civil War</u>

Volunteer Groups – Veteran Groups – Women's Christian
Temperance Union

<u>Progressive Movement</u>

Calling for reforms at railroads, anti-trust legislation, child labor
    Establishment of Food and Drug Administration (FDA)
in 1906
    Business regulation requires business involvement

Traditional Reputation of Lobbyists

The Nation Magazine: "somebody who is during one half of the
year without honest means of livelihood; and whose employment
by those who have bills before a legislature is only resorted to as a
disagreeable necessity"
    Pressure from some activists lead to reforms like child labor,
wages, hours of work, women's suffrage and business regulations
    Successful single-issue interest group = Anti-Saloon League.
Behind the 18th Amendment of banning alcohol

<u>19th century Dictionary of American Politics:</u>

Definition: "Lobby, The, is a term applied collectively to men that make a business of corruptly influencing legislators. Their object is usually accomplished by means of money paid to the members, but any means that is considered feasible is employed."

<u>Types of Interest Groups</u>

Interest groups vary greatly in their missions and memberships. Some are single-issue, others represent businesses and industry, others advocate the 'public interest'

The seize of these interest groups can range from millions to a handful of people

Three Categories: economic – public-interest – single-issue

Distinct Types of Public Interest Groups

<u>Citizen Groups</u>

Membership organizations open to all who agree with the policy goals of the organization. Tend to be ideological and idealistic

Mission is to act 'in the public interest', meaning to protect the rights, resources and liberties common to all Americans

<u>Examples:</u>

American Civil Liberties Union (ACLU): since 1st World War to strengthen Bill of Rights
    Public Citizen: Consumer Watchdog Group
    Public Interest Research Groups (PIRG): funded and controlled by college students
    Common Cause: voter registration, changing voting age
    Greenpeace, National Wildlife Federation

Social Movements

Informally organized, often temporary groups like 'Occupy Wall Street' or Civil Rights Movement
    This includes groups protesting a specific project like an airport or highway expansion

Distinct Types of Economic Interest Groups

<u>Purpose: to provide economic benefits to their members</u>

Corporations

Operate openly in the political arena to help shape policy that will enhance their profits

More than 750 corporations have offices in DC – for example Microsoft with 4 Vice-presidents and staff of more than 20 to deal with government relations

Labor Unions

Active in elections and have political staff in Washington

Broad policies that affect members like healthcare, taxes, workplace

Labor Unions: strongest union with 13 Million members = The American Federation of Labor and Congress of Industrial Organizations (AFL-CIO); Teamsters have 1.5 Million members and United Auto Workers have 800k members

Professional Associations

Lobby for benefits for their members or on behalf of issues that interfere with aspects of the specific profession

Because of "Free Riders" groups create 'selective benefits' for members. (Member advice, law and regulation education, training programs etc.)

National Association of Manufacturers: budget $25 Million; lobbying against Free Trade Agreements

Professional Associations: American Medical Association (AMA), Screen Actors Guild (SAG), American Bar Association (ABA)

Agricultural Associations

Lobbying for Farmers and farm related industries. Highly influential due to strong agricultural states and the importance of food production

American Farm Bureau Federation: 5 Million members, one of the oldest and most influential business lobbies

Trade Associations

Either trade businesses like Automobile Dealer or larger groups of businesses

U.S. Chamber of Commerce: 200,000 companies with annual dues of more than $30 Million

Distinct Types of Single-Issue Groups

Some of the most prominent and powerful interest groups

Extremely narrow and intense focus on an issue

Examples:

National Rights Action League (NARAL): keep abortion legal

Right to Live Committee: outlaw abortions

American Association of Retired People (AARP): 35 Million members and powerful. Started as insurance, now a service conglomerate for older people

National Rifle Association (NRA)

<u>Strategies and Tactics</u>

<u>Two categories direct and indirect</u>

<u>Direct Techniques</u>

Preferred method of influencing

Hiring specialized lobbying firms or retain lobbyists to gain access to decision makers

Former lobbyists and staff members are the best lobbyists. Due to continue privileges. Lobbying is not allowed for one year after leaving office (but many ways around it)

Interest groups have ratings on candidates and office holders, like NRA or American Conservative Union ACU

'Umbrella' organizations to unite resources

<u>Tools:</u>

Setting up private meetings with lawmakers to reveal their client's interest

Providing policy and political information

Drafting legislation

Testifying before Congressional committees on proposed legislation and rules

Interpreting the impact of proposed legislation

Organizing protest demonstrations

Campaign fundraisers for candidates; often done through a
<u>Political Action Committee</u> (PAC)
>   Talking to the media
>   Running ads in the media
>   Filing lawsuits or engaging in litigation

<u>Indirect Techniques</u>

Third party influencing
>   Used commonly is constituent lobbying, whereby members of
an organization write, phone and e-mail legislators
>   Kind of a grassroots lobbying that can be very effective
>   Public pressure through mass mailings, PR-campaigns and
demonstrations

<u>Regulating Lobbyists</u>

Federal Regulation of Lobbying Act (1946): first law to regulate
lobbying activity; provides public disclosure of lobbying activities.
It required lobbyists to register with the clerk of the House of
Representatives or the Secretary of the Senate to state their
purpose for lobbying, and provide quarterly updates on clients
and fees
>   <u>This law proved to be ineffective because of loopholes</u>

1954 Supreme Court: Act only applies to paid lobbyists whose
principal purpose is to influence Congress directly

Therefore, only about 7000 individuals and organizations registered

Lobbying Disclosure Act (1995)

Overhauling the Act with six new provisions:

- Defining lobbyists as anyone who spent more than 20% of her/his time lobbying members of Congress
- Banning for life former US trade representatives from lobbying for foreign interests
- Banning nonprofit groups that lobby from receiving federal grants
- Requiring semiannual reports disclosing specific issues, bills worked on and money spent
- Lawyers who represent foreign entities to register with Congress.
- Exemption for lobbyists who are paid less than $5000 semiannually

Influence over Foreign Policy

No lobbying of foreign governments. But ethnic American organization lobby Congress, like American Israel Public Affairs Committee (AIPAC) or Cuban American National Foundation (CANF)

Chapter 10

Media and Politics

~

WHAT YOU NEED TO KNOW

- **The Media plays a very important role in a democracy; they provide the transparency about government and politics**
- **Our system depends on free and open lines of communication**
- **How well the media performs these functions is affected by technological changes, government regulation and relationship between office holders and journalists**

Websites:

http://www.aim.org (accuracy in media)
http://www.newseum.org (500 front pages of major newspapers)

Question: What is the role and responsibility of the media in the democratic system?

Functions of the Media

Reporting and interpreting the news
    Helping to set the Public Agenda = filtering and framing
    Agent of Socialization = shaping norms, values and social roles
    Public forum = gatekeeping role
    Providing Entertainment
    Mediation ('Help me Howard')
    Service (traffic news)

Development of Media

Question: How has the media changed over time and what impact had these changes on the democratic process?

1700s first colonial newspaper

pamphlets influential for the revolution

'partisan press' = up to early 1800s the political parties control newspapers

'penny press' = newspapers sold for 1 penny, makes it affordable for masses

'yellow journalism' = reporting about sensations and other blaring stories

Telegraph

Radio (talk shows).

TV (cable stations)

New Media = Internet, new media, social media

Government Regulation of the Media

Question: Why does the government have greater power to regulate the broadcast media?

Regulating the Airways

1934 Communication Act created the Federal Communications Commission (FCC) to issue broadcast licenses

FCC has power to determine who can broadcast – authorized to issue, revoke or deny licenses

1996 Telecommunication Act = abolishes many cross-market barriers – leads to deregulation

FCC took steps to allow greater concentration of ownership (limit is 35% national audience)

Question of net neutrality? = unhindered flow of information

FCC requests fair, balanced coverage of public issues (content regulations)

Equal time rule (providing equal time to candidates)

Fairness Doctrine (reasonable time must be provided to discuss issues of community interest)

Fairness Doctrine stopped in 1987 – led to political talk radio.

<u>Cable and satellite transmissions are not subject to the same restrictions as traditional broadcast</u>

Regulating the Internet

1996 Congress passed the Communications Decency Act (indecent material). This was struck down by the Supreme Court in 1997 as 'too broad'

2000 Children's Internet Protection Act = regulates children access to internet in libraries, schools, filters

Important questions about <u>Net-Neutrality</u> and Consumer Information

Government and the Media

Question: Interaction between public officials and the media? How does Media cover events?

Officials try to 'spin' = influence how news is reported

Officials have created public relations infrastructure through which they provide information and access to reporters
Post of the Press Secretary of the White House or other institutions
Attempt to Control the Message

"Pack journalism" means that hordes of journalist cover the same even

<u>Realize how important the media is for the government or an incoming government. Election campaigns and its coverage are essential to win</u>

<u>Presidents and the Press</u>

Public support is a president's most valuable source of political power

<u>Talking Point:</u>
"See approval ratings for presidents as barometer for political power"

President Kennedy, master of televised press conferences
President Reagan, master of staging events
President Obama, master of being on all channels, Twitter 3 Million; Facebook 1.5 Million

·President Trump, master of being covered everywhere and to ignite controversies

Congress and the Press

The seize makes it difficult for the media to cover
   Since 1979 House of Representatives allows TV coverage of sessions (C Span)
   Since 1986 the Senate allows TV coverage of sessions (C Span)
   Members use the media to communicate with their constituents

Supreme Court and the Press

Far less covered than President or Congress
   Duties performed behind closed doors
   Since 2000 court issues audio recordings of aural arguments in high-profile cases

Elections

Media plays an important role in elections
   Experience the penetrations of coverage, news, ads during a presidential campaign
   Social Media more and more important, opens the door for misinformation and misguidance

Assessing the Media

Question: Is the Media bias and if so, how?

Media engages filtering and framing whenever they report the news

"Objective journalism" hard to achieve

60% of participants from a 2009 poll said that the news is bias; this percentage is probably higher today

29% felt that they get the 'facts right' in the same poll

Corporate interest of those who own the media versus journalistic truth. Editorial staff cannot report negatively about biggest advertiser

Personalization = tendency to downplay the big social and economic picture

Dramatization = issues presented as simple narratives that emphasize on crisis and personalities

Fragmentation = short, isolated stories

Chapter 11

Congress

∼

Statements

"Congress is and remains the 'first branch' of American government"

Congress is full of interesting political puzzles.
Reveals our democracy with legislative decision process, daily workings and organization

Still in line with the intention of the Framers not to have a "king" and to prevent a single "control of state"

R<u>easons why the system is working</u>

Powers and rights of Congress in Art. 1 of Constitution are strong
    Ultimate power of the purse (Budget)
    Congress can pass laws even if the president vetoes it
    Has oversight how laws are administered by the executive
    Can expand or contract the appellate jurisdiction of Supreme
Court

Elastic clause allows Congress to stretch institutional power by making laws supporting its role

But today

Congress is considered by many a 'broken branch'
    Public mistrust and 'we-them' perception
    Elite reform proposals, that bring no change

Models of Representation

Trustee Model

Representative follow their own convictions in making decisions

Delegate Model

Representatives should consult their constituents on pending issues

<u>Politico Model</u>

Sensitive to the needs of constituents, but relying on their own judgment

Congress moves slowly to incorporate all different aspects of congressional diversity. Goes against the American wish of clear action and strong leadership. Instead pulling and hauling before decisions (see the conflicts of the financial crisis and reaction of Congress)

<u>It is said, that the US has the only real legislative branch in any democracy (meaning Congress can exercise powers independently from executive branch)</u>

Bicameralism

Congress is a real two-chamber legislature with almost equal powers

 In other democracies, the second chamber has limited power, like House of Lords in the UK

 Makes policy making more time consuming and complex

<u>Difference between a Congress and Parliament</u>

Congress is from Latin, meaning 'a coming together'
　　Parliament is from French, meaning 'parler' = 'to talk'

In America, primaries decide if a candidate runs and not the party. A much stronger independence from the party. Congress is made of people chosen to represent their state and district rather than a common body for the 'common good'

In Parliament, most members are selected from lists provided by the parties. Government and the party or coalition members in parliament are much more intertwined. The chancellor or prime minister is elected out of the members of parliament

<u>Influence and Power of Congress</u>

A Representative had in 2000 a salary of about $150k plus all amenities. In addition, a staff of up to 22, privileges like 'franking privilege' and travel allowances

A member of Parliament is more poorly paid and treated due to party discipline.

<u>Talking Points:</u>

Are the members of Congress representative of the American people?

Reference to "Best Congress Money can buy" as statement for bias behavior

The House of Representatives

<u>"House is the closest to the people"</u>

Majority sets agenda and passions run high. Helps to understand the important public policy issues. A topic need to create a critical mass to be taken up by the house.

About 600,000 constituents per representative

Reelection every two years

Constituency casework required to be reelected

<u>"The Framers only intended to elect the House by the people"</u>

Leadership

Strict leadership needed for 435 different Representatives; leadership plays important role; organized by party

Speaker of the House

Current speaker of the House (2023): Kevin McCarthy (Rep.)

Most powerful and visible member of the House

Only House leadership specifically defined in the Constitution – third in line of presidential succession

Nominated by a majority of his party's caucus or membership in the house. At the beginning of each two-year session of Congress

Powers

- Determines committee assignments
- Preside over the House
- Decide on points of order and interpret the rule
- Refer legislation to the appropriate committees
- Set the agenda and schedule legislative action
- Coordinate policy agenda with Senate leadership and the President
- <u>"Speaker can be Friend or Enemy to the White House."</u>

Majority and Minority Leaders

Majority Leader

The principal deputy to the Speaker and floor leader of the majority party. Elected by secret ballot at the beginning of each two-year term

<u>Functions</u>

foster unity and cohesion among the members
    assist speaker in agenda setting, scheduling debates

Minority Leader

Leader of the opposition party
    Function similar regarding to keep unity
    Working together with Majority leader and Speaker to
determine rules of legislation
    No constitutional mandate

Whips

Majority and Minority leadership relies on 'whips", deputies who
are responsible for maintaining party loyalty and 'counting heads'
on key votes
    Whips are elected by secret ballot

Committees

Committees are the place for the real legislative work
    Members are confronted with a diversity of issues and
committees are established for Representatives to focus on their
key strength
    Every Member serves on two Standing Committees; House
Committees divided into 5 subcommittees

<u>Three primary types of Committees</u>

<u>Standing Committees</u>

- Appropriations
- Commerce
- Budget
- Ways and Means
- Banking and Financial Services

<u>Special Committees</u>

From time to time to study a particular issue and to create a report
   Joint Committees
      Committees for both House- and Senate Members

<u>Conference Committees</u>

House- and Senate Members try to find a common language for legislation

<u>Joining a Committee</u>

A committee assignment ranks among the most important aspects of the job as a congress member. Speaker and Minority leader determine the seat. Seniority plays an important role, but special knowledge or district needs are factors as well

Committee Leaders

Most powerful person is the chairperson. The chair hires majority staff, appoints subcommittee members and allocates the budgets

Rules

Large seize of house makes it necessary to be governed by strict rules
   Ruling debates with time restrictions and types of amendments allowed

Cliques and Caucuses

Outside of the formal leadership structure members can shape policy through participation in caucuses and alliances. Especially informal groups who band together over common ideas and interests

Most influential

Congressional Black Caucus (Democrats)
Freedom Caucus (Republicans)

To Run for House of Representatives

At least 25-years old
Resident of state in which your district resides
U.S. citizen for seven years

People

Incumbent candidate prone to win reelection
Forced through so called 'pork-barrel' = sending benefits home, meaning that public money is used for infrastructure or community projects
Earmarks = spending on projects authorized by Congress without undergoing the usual process of review. Can also mean tax breaks
2008: 14000 earmarks at $29 billion

Discussion about earmarks due to shady process, but 2009 only 0.5% of total budget

Demographic Representation

Members of Congress do not reflect the American population

Normal: white – end 50s – law degree – wealthier

Reality: African-American (8.1% representation to 12.6% of population nationwide) - Women (16.8% to 50.8% nationwide)

Hispanic (5.7% to 16.3% nationwide)

Descriptive representation = only reflecting view with same demographics

Substantive representation = support without sharing demographic characteristics

The Senate

Framers wanted this chamber to remain insulated from the popular passions of the day

Until 1913 senators were selected by their state legislatures

Since President Roosevelt Congress is less powerful, but still elitist

Two Special Rights

Authority to advise and consent on the president's appointments and treaties. At a single term about 35000 military and civilian appointments that require Senate confirmation. Confirmations are now more politicized; especially difficult hearings are for Supreme Court Judges

Conduct impeachment trials for federal officials. Exclusive domain over trial and conviction. Total of 16 Impeachment trials with seven convictions

Leadership

Different form of leadership, more collegial and informal with only 100 members

Vice President serves as Senate president and casts tie braking vote

Otherwise Senate President 'pro tempore' presides over chamber = member of the majority party and longest serving. He/she is also 4th in row to presidency

Majority and Minority Leaders

Committee Chairman very important in the 17 standing committees

Class A committees are "Judiciary", "Budget" and "Foreign Relations"

Filibuster

Practice of unlimited debate as distinguished right in the Senate

Filibustering = involves endless speech on the floor and other measures like delaying tactics

Highly effective mechanism to win concessions

They are rules of cutting a debate: When 3/5 of members present a vote to end debate, then they are 30 hours until final vote taken (cloture)

To run for Senate

Average campaign spends about $5 million (higher in CA, TX or NY).
  30 years' old
  Nine-year US-citizen and residing in state

Two Chambers Working Together

House in session from Tuesday through Thursday; other times in their districts
  Senate, the entire week
  Meetings, hearings, discussion about pending legislation
  Debate, Media, Meeting with government officials
  Constituent's work
  Political events and fundraisers
  Members have pager that alerts them 15 minutes before roll call

Congresswoman's Roles

Legislator
  Most important role. Each member casts thousands of votes each session
  Constituent Servant
  Intervene on behalf of their constituents; problem solving, promotion, commerce
  Representative

Dependency level on voters

<u>Educator</u>

Informing constituents and public in general through media and town hall meetings

<u>Making Decisions</u>

<u>Party Affiliation</u>

Majority of votes along party lines; best indicator of a member's vote

<u>Constituency</u>

Members take in account the views of their voters. Especially in high-profile issues

<u>Presidential Pressure</u>

Voting with the President in mind. Arm-twisting or popular persuasion

<u>Ideology</u>

Seldom, but splits across party lines

<u>Working with other Institutions</u>

<u>President</u>

Complex relationship; cooperation or confrontation depends on party majority

Balance has shifted towards the president

<u>The Courts</u>

Establishing federal court systems and confirming judicial

appointments
Creating more 'legislative intent' for the courts to consider

The Bureaucracy
Strong oversight capacity, including investigations and subpoena documents

The Role of Staff
10,000-plus staffers are working in the Capitol
The average Senator has about 35 staff members

Official Support System
Congressional Research Service (CRS)
Congressional Budget Office (CBO)
General Accounting

The Legislative Process

To become law, proposals must survive a complex, multi-step process that takes them through subcommittees and committees in both chambers

Aspects

Opponents have many opportunities to kill proposals
Differences between House and Senate
No single path by which bills become laws

Framers purposely established framework whereby lawmaking would be difficult

"Omnibus" bills cover a broad range of issues, used to speed up legislation process – more and more in use

Typically, legislators introduce a bill with support of co-sponsors

Process

1

Introduction

Member of congress introduces a bill, he/she needs support from fellow members

2

Committee Selection

The appropriate committee or committees are selected. Committee consideration with hearings and witnesses to the matter. "Mark up phase" to debate the final language

3

Scheduling

The calendar is an important aspect to determine the order of bills. In the House, they are four types of calendars that handle different kinds of legislation. In the Senate, they are two calendars for executive and legislative actions. In the House, the Rules Committee controls the calendar; in the Senate, the Majority and Minority Leader are setting the schedule together

4

Floor action (closed rule, open rule and Riders)

House Rules Committee is influential, by announcing the floor rule action of the bill. It needs a majority in the House for the bill to go to the floor for debate. At this time, requested amendments are added. The final vote is done with an electronic device and selects 'yes', 'no', and 'present'

5

Conference Committee

To find a final agreement between House and Senate on the version of the bill is essential. The conference committee oversees this task. Both versions of the bill (House and Senate) must be identical

Normally a coordination process is in place during each legislation. For differences in the versions, the conference committees is put in place to hammer out a deal

6

<u>Presidential Action (enrolled bills)</u>

The president can sign a bill into law or veto it. The presidential veto can be overridden with 2/3 in each chamber. This scenario is rare; only 5% of vetoes were overridden by Congress

The president can choose not to act on a bill. He may decide neither to sign nor veto a bill. If Congress is in session, the bill becomes law after ten days without the president's signature. Otherwise, the bill suffers a pocket veto and does not become law

Fast Track Legislation possible in situation of danger or the necessity to act decisively

Chapter 12

Presidency

∾

Statement

**"Although Congress was intended to be the 'first branch'
among American Institutions, the presidency has
supplanted it as the focal point of our system over the
course of 200 years. A combination of personalities and
events has reshaped the office into the modern
presidency."**

P residential and Parliamentary Systems

In a presidential system, the president is elected directly. A prime minister or chancellor belong to the strongest party or coalition in parliament and are much more dependent

The Office

<u>The powers of the president are expressed in Art.2 of the Constitution:</u>

<u>Military</u>

Commander in Chief - Commission of high ranking officers
Congress normally declares war; this was last done in 1941. This means, that Congress never declared war in Korea or Vietnam. So far, Congress has passed resolutions, approving the president's action
Military powers can be exercised domestically
1973 Congress passed "War Powers Resolution". It reaffirms that presidents can only send troops into action with authorization of Congress
Presidents claim inherent executive power to defend the nation

<u>Judicial</u>

The president has the power to grant reprieves, pardons and amnesties

This involves the power of life or death over individuals by ordering assassinations

Diplomatic

Chief Representative in dealings with other nations
Receives ambassadors
Power to make treaties, but needs the consent of the Senate
Avoiding Congress approval by calling it an "executive agreement"
Power to recognize other countries

Executive

Chief Executive. Important basis of the president's power as chief executive is the stipulation in the Constitution that the President "makes sure that all laws are faithfully executed"
Inherent Powers of the President = in times of war and emergency. President claims powers not expressed in the Constitution. Evolved out of the phrase: "rights, duties and obligations of the presidency"

President's 'assumption of emergency powers' is a so-called 'loaded gun' by assuming unprecedented powers:
Abraham Lincoln's executive orders in the Civil War
World War II and treatment of Japanese Americans
9/11 and war against terrorism

Additional executive powers

The power to appoint or remove and supervise all executive officers and all federal judges. Especially important for the Supreme Court

Legislative

Veto power

pocket veto = Congress must introduce the bill in next session through 10-day inaction of the President

"State of the Union" address as a recommendation what kind of legislation shall be taken up in Congress (this right has developed with the stronger personality/role of Presidents)

Not constitutional is the president's ability to initiate legislative action

Executive Orders

A way for the president to create a procedure that acts in place of congressional authorization. Used often in times when the opposing party to the president has a majority in Congress

Synopsis

Historically, the powers of the president were not merely given, but developed out of necessity, personal ambitions and changing perceptions.

Delegation of Power from Congress to Presidency

President "… shall take care that the Laws be faithfully executed …" means that Congress delegates to the President the power to implement its will = delegated powers

Presidents have achieved to capture these delegated powers

Congress has voluntarily delegated a great deal of its own legislative authority to the executive branch

Expanded administrative activities since the New Deal

Examples are the establishment of the Department of Homeland Security with many powers or The EPA becoming the power to enforce air-and water quality standards

Election process historically

Fight between the Framers about the position of the president. This leads to an indirect election through an electoral college. The electors were first selected by state legislators

This procedure dampens the power of Presidents in the 19th century

Direct elections of the electorate lead to an increased power of the presidents

The Presidency stands apart for many reasons

Only nationally elected office
    Only term-limited position
    Office is greater than the sum of its constitutional parts
    'Commander in Chief'
    'Chief Executive'
    'Chief Legislator'
    'Chief Diplomat'
    'Head of State'
    'Chief Budgeter'
    'Chief Communicator'.
    Leader of the Free World and Commander of the Worlds
Superpower (1/3 of world defense budget)
    Commands the nation's attention
    No matter if voted for or not, the president is the president
of all

Institutional Resources of Presidential Power

Formal and informal resources that have important implications
for the ability to govern. More informal resources available
    Cabinet is the traditional but informal designation for the
heads of all the major federal government departments. Cabinet
Secretaries are appointed by the president with consent of the
Senate
    Cabinet has no constitutional status – 15 today
    American Cabinet does not make decisions as a group, no
collective responsibility = difference to other governments

Cabinet takes on important responsibilities in communication with the president

"groupthink" phenomena to agree more within the group, losing critical distance

Independent Agencies

These federal agencies are not considered part of the president's cabinet. The president cannot remove members of these agencies due to a fixed term

Examples:

Federal Reserve Board (12y)
Consumer Product Safety Commission (6y)
Federal Trade Commission (7y)

The White House Staff

The White House Staff are analysts and advisers who are closest to the president's needs and preferences. Normally closely politically related

Daily access to the president – White house Chief of Staff most important; coordinates the flow to the Oval Office

The Executive Office of the President (EOP) is the permanent agencies that perform defined management tasks for the president. Created in 1939 the EOP includes the Office of Management and

Budget OMB), the Council of Economic Advisers CEA) and the National Security Council (NSC)

Executive Office of the President (EOP)

EOP is a major part of what is often called the 'institutional presidency'

Around 500 people working in the EOP

Some write speeches, work with Congress, political advice, meetings, public appearances

Providing information for the president – complex situations require many resources

The Vice President

The Vice President has become more important since the 1970s. The office exists for 2 purposes:

to succeed the president

to preside over Senate

Electoral importance for the president, meaning that the 'running mate' can capture votes that the president cannot

The First Lady

The First Lady has no constitutional role, but plays an important role anyway. Every first lady tries to pick a theme to concentrate in the social field, like Michelle Obama with Health and Fitness for Children, Melania Trump against Cyber-bullying, and Jill Biden's initiative for education

Administrative Strategy – Presidents and Bureaucracy

Presidents do not control the executive branch
Congress determines the organization of the federal bureaucracy, establishes budget, right to control personnel, guiding federal programs
Presidents are 'reigning, but not ruling'

Presidents can though advance their programs using an administrative strategy:

The president has the executive interpretation of how, if or when to apply the laws
Details about the administrative approach are very important
Broad legislative goals need to be translated in concrete programs

Executive Orders

Presidential Proclamations help accomplish goals without congressional approval. "Govern by decree"

<u>Judicial Strategy – Presidents and the Courts</u>

Selecting like-minded nominee for the federal courts
    Federal and Supreme Court Judges are a legacy for the
president

<u>Enforcing federal laws delegated to Department of Justice, acting
independently</u>

Chapter 13

Bureaucracy

~

Synopsis

Americans depend on the government bureaucracies to accomplish daily life. We rely on these government services every day and especially in emergencies Bureaucracies provide essential services. And yet, they are looked upon with scrutiny and distrust in the public. "Bureau" = French for office or desk; "Cracy"= Greek for rule

D<u>efinition</u>

"Bureaucracy is the complex structures of offices, tasks, rules, and principals of organization that are employed by all large-scale institutions to coordinate effectively the work of their personnel."

Thesis

"when an organization is inefficient, it is almost certainly because it is not bureaucratic enough"

Bureaucracies perform specialized tasks and routine actions to do their job effectively. The bureaucrats require resources and tools ("paper to blood samples"). They must coordinate their work with others (contractors) and effectively outreach to the public (health warnings)

Talking Point:

Has the word 'Bureaucracy' a positive or negative connotation?

Services we use daily

- We check the weather forecast – U.S. Weather Service
- Drive on Interstate Highway – Department of Transportation
- Mail a check – U.S. Postal Service
- Drink from public fountain – EPA
- Check the ingredient list on a product – FDA
- Attend a class – Student loan program of the U.S. Dep. of Education
- Check emails – Advance Research Projects Agency
- Meet somebody at the airport – Federal Aviation Administration

<u>Disasters:</u> FEMA

Seize

Different ideas about the size of government. In general, Democrats more prone to 'big' government. Libertarian position as little government as possible

  1968 peak with 3 Million civilian employees plus 3.6 Million military

  2008 around 2.7 Mil civilian and 1.4 Mil military

  Ratio between private and public sector in 2007 around 14%

Roles

Bureaucracy fills in the blanks by determining how laws shall be interpreted and executed

  Bureaucracy have much more specialized expertise in specific policy areas than members of Congress

  Bureaucracy issue rules – rule making is a form of legislation, a "quasi-legislation" (see EPA)

  Bureaucracy enforce the laws (see Product Safety Commission and producers of toys or cars)

Bureaucracy Policy Making

<u>Iron Triangle</u>

Alliance formed by Congress, Bureaucracy and Interest Groups
    Reason: Congress receives campaign contribution; interest groups get favorable legislation and Bureaucracy preserves jobs and influence
    "Captured Agency" = agency makes rules favorable to interest groups although they should regulate them

Who are the Bureaucrats?

90% of federal work force are career civil servants
    Retain position regardless who is governing
    Political appointees for the top positions
    Office of Personnel Management (OPM) recruits and interviews potential civil servants
    Until 1900s all government jobs were political, payback time
    Merit System for Bureaucracy = less money, but job security, pensions, health insurance
    Leads to a certain kind of people that go for these careers.

Features of Modern Bureaucracy
Weber's Model of Bureaucracy

German sociologist who wrote about the historical evolution of administrative systems at the turn of the 20th century

Five qualities as functional features of Bureaucracy

- Hierarchy of authority: pyramid structure
- System of Rules: used to guide decisions
- Division and specialization of labor: those with expertise will be responsible
- Written records: extensive record-keeping
- Careers based on merit: rising in the hierarchy due to personal ability

Five Factors that are dysfunctional features of Bureaucracy

- Understanding fades up the ladder: those on top know less about a problem
- Decisions based on rules: ignoring unique problems
- Specialization can blur big picture: commitment to more immediate goals
- Written records delay responses
- Career officials value future benefits over current productivity: looking to spent time until retirement

Distinctive Features of U.S. Bureaucracy

"The political authority of Bureaucracy is not in one set of hands but is shared among several institutions."

President and Congress exercise authority over Bureaucracy (difference to parliamentary system)

Uncertain guidance if President and Congress are divided (difference to parliamentary system)

Two masters in the executive and legislative branch

Divided authority encourages Bureaucracy to play one branch against another and use media

Bureaucracy shares functions on federal, state and local level

Related bureaucratic agencies on all levels. They need to work together to implement programs and spend money

Bureaucrats are under close observation by citizens

Strong Cultural Distrust

Americans skeptical about programs operated by government officials

"bureaucratic" as a term for slow and inefficient

2009 poll said that people believe of $1, 50cents are wasted when government takes control

Privatization in the U.S. was the first and most complete and Europe followed

Bureaucratic Structures

Not a single set of organization, but different arrangements and procedures. Work between different overlapping agencies

The implementation of the Department of Homeland Security as attempt to streamline different security agencies

Getting appointed

After every presidential election, the Government Printing Office (GPO) publishes 'United States Government Policy and Supporting Positions ("the plum book") for all available positions

Because Senate needs to approve appointments, many positions remain empty for weeks and months. This has increased due to increased partisanship

Most appointees remain two to three years in office

Tendency among bureaucrats to disregard their supervisor's policies; only 0.1% of civil servants fired per year; slow to bring Bureaucracy under control and to implement change

Controlling the Bureaucracy

Assumption that bureaucracy and democracy are contradictory. Task is neither to retreat from Bureaucracy nor to attack it, but to take advantage of its strengths while making it more accountable to the demands of democratic politics = <u>Administrative Accountability</u>

Bureaucratic Agencies regulate the economy. In the process Congress delegated some authority to the executive branch. Congress tries to find ways in controlling the executive branch while losing authority to it

Bureaucracy resists, but does not confront

Pulling the Purse Strings

The Congress oversees Bureaucracy with the authorization and appropriations process

There is permanent authorization, like Social Security Administration and NASA

President brings Budget to Congress with the help of the Office of Management and Budget (OMB) and Congress controls it with help of the General Accounting Office (GAO)

Authorization of Programs

President has system of <u>central clearance</u> = revue of agencies' program ideas and proposals performed by the OMB

Non-Appropriations Methods

Hearings and Investigations: asking agencies to testify before Congress committees, Government Accounting Office (GAO) and Congressional Budget Office (CBO)

Oversight over programs and monitoring progress by Congress

Mandatory reports: requests from Congress to periodically assess programs and report their findings; allows Congress to find out how a law is effective

Inspectors general: every agency has inspector general (IGs) who reside outside the Bureaucracy chain of command; IGs report to Congress and perform specific investigations

Whistleblowers

Bringing attention to an illegal or corrupt behavior
Whistleblowers play an important role in agency oversight
Examples: "Deep Throat/Watergate", Eric Snowden/NSA

Four Types of Structures in the Federal Bureaucracy

1

Cabinet or Executive Departments = Administration

15 Departments in total (structure of a Department from 'Secretary' down)
Creation of a department as a major national commitment (Dep. of Homeland Security 2002 and 1965 Housing and Urban Development).

2

Independent Executive Agencies

Congress created the number of federal agencies to delegate power to the Bureaucracy and enforcing regulations
Located outside the cabinet structure
Agencies report directly to president
Remain independent to do the job
Environmental Protection Agency (EPA), Peace Corps, Small Business Administration (SBA)

3

Independent Regulatory Commissions

Created with the purpose of regulating sectors of the economy
Totally independent from President and Congress, not part of an executive department
Congress delegates its oversight to these agencies and not to executive branch
Run by board of commissioners, appointed for fixed terms, confirmed by Senate
Federal Reserve Board of Governors
Securities and Exchange Commission
Equal Employment Opportunity Commission

4

Government Corporations

Established by Congress
"to perform a public purpose, provide a market-oriented service and produce revenues to meet at least its expenditures."

Quasi-governmental agencies

Created when the government's activity is commercial in nature
Behave like private companies and generate revenues (board of directors)
No public shareholders
USPS (900,000 employees)

Amtrak
Export-Import Bank
Federal Deposit Insurance Corporation (FDIC)
Other Forms of Government Corporations = Government
Sponsored Entities (GSEs)

Shareholder owned companies, created by federal government

Federal National Mortgage Ass. (Fannie Mae)
  Federal Home Loan Mortgage Corporation (Freddie Mac)
  Student Loan Marketing Ass. (Sallie Mae)

Attempts at Reform

Complaints about inefficiency, ineffectiveness, arrogance, lack of
responsiveness to the public needs
  Bureaucracy ranks among the most unpopular institutions
  Congress attempted several times to reform Bureaucracy
  Sunshine Act of 1976 requires that federal agencies hold their
meetings open to the public
  States have created "sunset laws" to gain greater control.
Allowing bureaucratic agencies to be terminated at the end of a
designated period

Privatization

More and more public services get privatized. Especially Prisons, Schools, Waste- and Water Management, Security Functions offer great incentives for private business

Chapter 14

Judiciary System

YOU NEED TO KNOW

- **Third branch of government, part of checks and balances**
- **Congress establishes federal courts**
- **President appoints federal judges and Supreme Court judges**
- **Lifetime assignment of judges**
- **Judiciary power is the power by the Supreme Court to find laws constitutional or not**

Proceeding of the federal judiciary is not well known. Reason is that proceedings aren't covered by the press with the same intensity like the other branches

Most disputes are handled at the state court level
Role and Procedures can seem complex and confusing

History of the Federal Judiciary

Differences over the shape of Judiciary.
Federalists: creating trial courts, appellate courts and one supreme tribunal.
Antifederalists: state courts serve as trial and appellate courts and national supreme court hears final appeal.

Compromise in Article 3 of the Constitution

"The judicial Power of the United States shall be vested in one supreme Court, and in such inferior Courts as the Congress may from time to time ordain and establish"

This mandate to the Congress needed to be resolved. Done with:

Judiciary Act of 1789

Three-tier federal judiciary by adding a trial and appellate level, but limiting the jurisdiction of the federal courts
State courts have jurisdiction over federal issues

Sources of American Law

<u>American law comes from a variety of sources:</u>

Federal and State Constitutions
    Federal and State Statues and Acts
    Case law

1

Federal and State Constitutions

Constitution is the supreme law of the land. No law can contravene it

    Constitution establishes a guideline by which all federal and state laws must adhere

    Supreme Court has compiled a vast body of constitutional law based on its interpretation of the Constitution

    Interpretations have varied from court to court. It shows how law evolves over time

    Highest court in each state interprets its state's constitution

2

Statues and Acts

Legislative acts are growing area of American law

Thousands of legislative bodies promulgate new laws and regulations (zoning rules, highway speed, hazardous waste etc.)

Legislative bodies are Congress, state legislators, county-, municipal- and district governments (50k people in a legislative capacity)

"Stare decisis" = "let the decision stand" means that courts follow earlier rulings when deciding a case

3

Case Law

Decisions by courts have formed a body of law referred to as "case law"

Case law is found in court opinions; tradition from England

Case law differs from statutory law in that it is flexible, and can evolve over time to reflect changes in society

Case law makes the Constitution a 'living document'

Power of Judicial Review = Constitutional Review

Theory: Job of the courts to interpret and apply the law

Reality: Judges make policy

Judicial Review is the authority of the courts to determine whether acts of Congress, executive branch and states are constitutional.

But this concept is not in the Constitution; it was established in the case Marbury versus Madison

Case Marbury vs Madison

John Adams appointed William Marbury as federal justice of the peace. New president James Madison refuses to recognize this appointment

Supreme Court justice John Marshall wants to recognize appointment, but knows that Madison will ignore decision and will weaken the court

His Ruling: Supreme Court cannot hear the case, because the Judiciary Act of 1789 allowing to hear these cases is unconstitutional

Supremacy clause affirms the Supreme Court right to review the constitutionality of state laws

Important to have states comply with laws (air pollution, voting rights)

Supreme Court cannot hear a case involving judicial review, if there is nobody injured

·All courts have the power to determine the constitutionality of legislative acts

This is different to other democracies where only the highest court can determine constitutionality

Judicial Activism and Restraint

"Activist Judges" = believe for courts to use aggressively judicial review. This approach is linked with political liberalism

"Restraint Judges" = accept more the judgment of the elected branches and is connected to conservatism

The Federal Court System

The Federal court system is organized like a pyramid. On top is the Supreme Court followed by an Appellate court level just below and the district (trial) courts at the base. The power flows downward

<u>District Courts</u>

They are the starting point into the federal judicial system.

Created by the Judiciary Act of 1789, the 94 district courts (with more than 600 judges) are the trial courts for the federal judiciary

Every state, incl. DC, Guam, Puerto Rico, Virgin Islands, has at least one district court and larger states have several (CA, TX, NY with four)

<u>Three Types of Cases</u>

1

Criminal matters initiated by the U.S. attorney for that district. Federal income tax evasion and counterfeiting U.S. currency. Trafficking narcotics over state lines

2

Civil cases if the dispute is based on matters of civil law (copyright, trademark infringement)

3

Public law cases suing governmental agencies

Court of Appeals (Appellate Court)

The losing party at the district court can appeal at the U.S. court of appeals

Appellate courts divided among 13 geographic circuits

Appellate courts cannot refuse cases, review questions of law and not questions of fact

Appellate court's ruling is rarely overturned, because Supreme Court takes very few cases

13th Federal Circuit has no geographic jurisdiction, instead nationwide jurisdiction over federal policy like patents or actions where the US government is the defendant

Getting into Federal Court

No automatic right to appear in federal court

Most cases occur in state courts

Two requirements necessary: Jurisdiction and Standing

Question of Jurisdiction

Type 1

Federal courts composed of limited jurisdiction, meaning it can only hear cases where it has express authority to do so. This federal question can derive from the Constitution, an act of Congress, an executive branch ruling or treaty disputes

Type 2

Litigating parties are citizens of different states
    Amount exceeds $75k

Type 3

Disputes between U.S. citizens and foreign governments

Question of Standing

To sue in federal court, the 'moving party' (bringing lawsuit) must have legal standing
    Standing is another way of saying that the litigant is entitled to appear before the court

Four Conditions must be present

There must be a conflict

Plaintiff must have been harmed and there must be a remedy

Issue cannot be "moot" = meaning that the case was resolved already (no merit ruling)

Specific plea alleged in the complaint, specific violation of the law

Chapter 15

The Constitution

~

(**P**reamble)

We the People of the United States, in Order to form a more perfect Union, establish Justice, insure domestic Tranquility, provide for the common defense, promote the general Welfare, and secure the Blessings of Liberty to ourselves and our Posterity, do ordain and establish this Constitution for the United States of America.

Article I (Article 1 - Legislative)

Section 1

All legislative Powers herein granted shall be vested in a Congress of the United States, which shall consist of a Senate and House of Representatives.

Section 2

1: The House of Representatives shall be composed of Members chosen every second Year by the People of the several States, and the Electors in each State shall have the Qualifications requisite for Electors of the most numerous Branch of the State Legislature.

2: No Person shall be a Representative who shall not have attained to the Age of twenty five Years, and been seven Years a Citizen of the United States, and who shall not, when elected, be an Inhabitant of that State in which he shall be chosen.

3: Representatives and direct Taxes shall be apportioned among the several States which may be included within this Union, according to their respective Numbers, which shall be determined by adding to the whole Number of free Persons, including those bound to Service for a Term of Years, and excluding Indians not taxed, three fifths of all other Persons.[2] The actual Enumeration shall be made within three Years after the first Meeting of the Congress of the United States, and within every subsequent Term of ten Years, in such Manner as they shall by Law direct. The Number of Representatives shall not exceed one for every thirty Thousand, but each State shall have at Least one Representative; and until such enumeration shall be made, the State of New Hampshire shall be entitled to choose three, Massachusetts eight, Rhode-Island and

Providence Plantations one, Connecticut five, New-York six, New Jersey four, Pennsylvania eight, Delaware one, Maryland six, Virginia ten, North Carolina five, South Carolina five, and Georgia three.

4: When vacancies happen in the Representation from any State, the Executive Authority thereof shall issue Writs of Election to fill such Vacancies.

5: The House of Representatives shall choose their Speaker and other Officers; and shall have the sole Power of Impeachment.

Section 3

1: The Senate of the United States shall be composed of two Senators from each State, chosen by the Legislature thereof, for six Years; and each Senator shall have one Vote.

2: Immediately after they shall be assembled in Consequence of the first Election, they shall be divided as equally as may be into three Classes. The Seats of the Senators of the first Class shall be vacated at the Expiration of the second Year, of the second Class at the Expiration of the fourth Year, and of the third Class at the Expiration of the sixth Year, so that one third may be chosen every second Year; and if Vacancies happen by Resignation, or otherwise, during the Recess of the Legislature of any State, the Executive thereof may make temporary Appointments until the next Meeting of the Legislature, which shall then fill such Vacancies.[4]

3: No Person shall be a Senator who shall not have attained to the Age of thirty Years, and been nine Years a Citizen of the United States, and who shall not, when elected, be an Inhabitant of that State for which he shall be chosen.

4: The Vice President of the United States shall be President of the Senate, but shall have no Vote, unless they be equally divided.

5: The Senate shall choose their other Officers, and also a President pro tempore, in the Absence of the Vice President, or when he shall exercise the Office of President of the United States.

6: The Senate shall have the sole Power to try all Impeachments. When sitting for that Purpose, they shall be on Oath or Affirmation. When the President of the United States is tried, the Chief Justice shall preside: And no Person shall be convicted without the Concurrence of two thirds of the Members present.

7: Judgment in Cases of impeachment shall not extend further than to removal from Office, and disqualification to hold and enjoy any Office of honor, Trust or Profit under the United States: but the Party convicted shall nevertheless be liable and subject to Indictment, Trial, Judgment and Punishment, according to Law.

Section 4

1: The Times, Places and Manner of holding Elections for Senators and Representatives, shall be prescribed in each State by the Legislature thereof; but the Congress may at any time by Law make or alter such Regulations, except as to the Places of choosing Senators.

2: The Congress shall assemble at least once in every Year, and such Meeting shall be on the first Monday in December, unless they shall by Law appoint a different Day.

Section 5

1: Each House shall be the Judge of the Elections, Returns and Qualifications of its own Members, and a Majority of each shall constitute a Quorum to do Business; but a smaller Number may adjourn from day to day, and may be authorized to compel the Attendance of absent Members, in such Manner, and under such Penalties as each House may provide.

2: Each House may determine the Rules of its Proceedings, punish its Members for disorderly Behavior, and, with theConcurrence of two thirds, expel a Member.

3: Each House shall keep a Journal of its Proceedings, and from time to time publish the same, excepting such Parts as may in their Judgment require Secrecy; and the Yeas and Nays of the Members of either House on any question shall, at the Desire of one fifth of those Present, be entered on the Journal.

4: Neither House, during the Session of Congress, shall, without the Consent of the other, adjourn for more than three days, nor to any other Place than that in which the two Houses shall be sitting.

Section 6

1: The Senators and Representatives shall receive a Compensation for their Services, to be ascertained by Law, and paid out of the Treasury of the United States. They shall in all Cases, except Treason, Felony and Breach of the Peace, be privileged from Arrest during their Attendance at the Session of their respective Houses, and in going to and returning from the same; and for any Speech or Debate in either House, they shall not be questioned in any other Place.

2: No Senator or Representative shall, during the Time for which he was elected, be appointed to any civil Office under the

Authority of the United States, which shall have been created, or the Emoluments whereof shall have been increased during such time; and no Person holding any Office under the United States, shall be a Member of either House during his Continuance in Office.

Section 7

1: All Bills for raising Revenue shall originate in the House of Representatives; but the Senate may propose or concur with Amendments as on other Bills.

2: Every Bill which shall have passed the House of Representatives and the Senate, shall, before it become a Law, be presented to the President of the United States; If he approve he shall sign it, but if not he shall return it, with his Objections to that House in which it shall have originated, who shall enter the Objections at large on their Journal, and proceed to reconsider it. If after such Reconsideration two thirds of that House shall agree to pass the Bill, it shall be sent, together with the Objections, to the other House, by which it shall likewise be reconsidered, and if approved by two thirds of that House, it shall become a Law. But in all such Cases the Votes of both Houses shall be determined by yeas and Nays, and the Names of the Persons voting for and against the Bill shall be entered on the Journal of each House respectively. If any Bill shall not be returned by the President within ten Days (Sundays excepted) after it shall have been presented to him, the Same shall be a Law, in like Manner as if he had signed it, unless the Congress by their Adjournment prevent its Return, in which Case it shall not be a Law.

3: Every Order, Resolution, or Vote to which the Concurrence of the Senate and House of Representatives may be necessary (except on a question of Adjournment) shall be presented to the President of the United States; and before the Same shall take Effect, shall be approved by him, or being disapproved by him, shall be repassed by two thirds of the Senate and House of Representatives, according to the Rules and Limitations prescribed in the Case of a Bill.

Section 8

1: The Congress shall have Power To lay and collect Taxes, Duties, Imposts and Excises, to pay the Debts and provide for the common Defence and general Welfare of the United States; but all Duties, Imposts and Excises shall be uniform throughout the United States;

2: To borrow Money on the credit of the United States;

3: To regulate Commerce with foreign Nations, and among the several States, and with the Indian Tribes;

4: To establish an uniform Rule of Naturalization, and uniform Laws on the subject of Bankruptcies throughout the United States;

5: To coin Money, regulate the Value thereof, and of foreign Coin, and fix the Standard of Weights and Measures;

6: To provide for the Punishment of counterfeiting the Securities and current Coin of the United States;

7: To establish Post Offices and post Roads;

8: To promote the Progress of Science and useful Arts, by securing for limited Times to Authors and Inventors the exclusive Right to their respective Writings and Discoveries;

9: To constitute Tribunals inferior to the supreme Court;

10: To define and punish Piracies and Felonies committed on the high Seas, and Offenses against the Law of Nations;

11: To declare War, grant Letters of Marque and Reprisal, and make Rules concerning Captures on Land and Water;

12: To raise and support Armies, but no Appropriation of Money to that Use shall be for a longer Term than two Years;

13: To provide and maintain a Navy;

14: To make Rules for the Government and Regulation of the land and naval Forces;

15: To provide for calling forth the Militia to execute the Laws of the Union, suppress Insurrections and repel Invasions;

16: To provide for organizing, arming, and disciplining, the Militia, and for governing such Part of them as may be employed in the Service of the United States, reserving to the States respectively, the Appointment of the Officers, and the Authority of training the Militia according to the discipline prescribed by Congress;

17: To exercise exclusive Legislation in all Cases whatsoever, over such District (not exceeding ten Miles square) as may, by Cession of particular States, and the Acceptance of Congress, become the Seat of the Government of the United States, and to exercise like Authority over all Places purchased by the Consent of the Legislature of the State in which the Same shall be, for the Erection of Forts, Magazines, Arsenals, dock-Yards, and other needful Buildings;—And

18: To make all Laws which shall be necessary and proper for carrying into Execution the foregoing Powers, and all other Powers vested by this Constitution in the Government of the United States, or in any Department or Officer thereof.

Section 9

1: The Migration or Importation of such Persons as any of the States now existing shall think proper to admit, shall not be prohibited by the Congress prior to the Year one thousand eight hundred and eight, but a Tax or duty may be imposed on such Importation, not exceeding ten dollars for each Person.

2: The Privilege of the Writ of Habeas Corpus shall not be suspended, unless when in Cases of Rebellion or Invasion the public Safety may require it.

3: No Bill of Attainder or ex post facto Law shall be passed.

4: No Capitation, or other direct, Tax shall be laid, unless in Proportion to the Census or Enumeration herein before directed to be taken.[7]

5: No Tax or Duty shall be laid on Articles exported from any State.

6: No Preference shall be given by any Regulation of Commerce or Revenue to the Ports of one State over those of another: nor shall Vessels bound to, or from, one State, be obliged to enter, clear, or pay Duties in another.

7: No Money shall be drawn from the Treasury, but in Consequence of Appropriations made by Law; and a regular Statement and Account of the Receipts and Expenditures of all public Money shall be published from time to time.

8: No Title of Nobility shall be granted by the United States: And no Person holding any Office of Profit or Trust under them, shall, without the Consent of the Congress, accept of any present, Emolument, Office, or Title, of any kind whatever, from any King, Prince, or foreign State.

Section 10

1: No State shall enter into any Treaty, Alliance, or Confederation; grant Letters of Marque and Reprisal; coin Money; emit Bills of Credit; make any Thing but gold and silver Coin a Tender in Payment of Debts; pass any Bill of Attainder, ex post facto Law, or Law impairing the Obligation of Contracts, or grant any Title of Nobility.

2: No State shall, without the Consent of the Congress, lay any Imposts or Duties on Imports or Exports, except what may be absolutely necessary for executing it's inspection Laws: and the net Produce of all Duties and Imposts, laid by any State on Imports or Exports, shall be for the Use of the Treasury of the United States; and all such Laws shall be subject to the Revision and Control of the Congress.

3: No State shall, without the Consent of Congress, lay any Duty of Tonnage, keep Troops, or Ships of War in time of Peace, enter into any Agreement or Compact with another State, or with a foreign Power, or engage in War, unless actually invaded, or in such imminent Danger as will not admit of delay.

Article II (Article 2 - Executive)

Section 1

1: The executive Power shall be vested in a President of the United States of America. He shall hold his Office during the Term of four Years, and, together with the Vice President, chosen for the same Term, be elected, as follows

2: Each State shall appoint, in such Manner as the Legislature thereof may direct, a Number of Electors, equal to the whole Number of Senators and Representatives to which the State may be entitled in the Congress: but no Senator or Representative, or Person holding an Office of Trust or Profit under the United States, shall be appointed an Elector.

3: The Electors shall meet in their respective States, and vote by Ballot for two Persons, of whom one at least shall not be an Inhabitant of the same State with themselves. And they shall make a List of all the Persons voted for, and of the Number of Votes for each; which List they shall sign and certify, and transmit sealed to the Seat of the Government of the United States, directed to the President of the Senate. The President of the Senate shall, in the Presence of the Senate and House of Representatives, open all the Certificates, and the Votes shall then be counted. The Person having the greatest Number of Votes shall be the President, if such Number be a Majority of the whole Number of Electors appointed; and if there be more than one who have such Majority, and have an equal Number of Votes, then the House of Representatives shall immediately choose by Ballot one of them for President; and if no Person have a Majority, then from the five highest on the List the said House shall in like Manner choose the President. But in choosing the President, the Votes shall be taken by States, the Representation from each State having one Vote; A quorum for this Purpose shall consist of a Member or Members from two thirds of the States, and a Majority of all the States shall be necessary to a Choice. In every Case, after the Choice of the President, the Person having the greatest Number of Votes of the Electors shall be the Vice President. But if there should remain two or more who have equal Votes, the Senate shall choose from them by Ballot the Vice President.[8]

4: The Congress may determine the Time of choosing the Electors, and the Day on which they shall give their Votes; which Day shall be the same throughout the United States.

5: No Person except a natural born Citizen, or a Citizen of the United States, at the time of the Adoption of this Constitution, shall be eligible to the Office of President; neither shall any Person be eligible to that Office who shall not have attained to the Age of thirty five Years, and been fourteen Years a Resident within the United States.

6: In Case of the Removal of the President from Office, or of his Death, Resignation, or Inability to discharge the Powers and Duties of the said Office,[9] the Same shall devolve on the Vice President, and the Congress may by Law provide for the Case of Removal, Death, Resignation or Inability, both of the President and Vice President, declaring what Officer shall then act as President, and such Officer shall act accordingly, until the Disability be removed, or a President shall be elected.

7: The President shall, at stated Times, receive for his Services, a Compensation, which shall neither be increased nor diminished during the Period for which he shall have been elected, and he shall not receive within that Period any other Emolument from the United States, or any of them.

8: Before he enter on the Execution of his Office, he shall take the following Oath or Affirmation:—"I do solemnly swear (or affirm) that I will faithfully execute the Office of President of the United States, and will to the best of my Ability, preserve, protect and defend the Constitution of the United States."

Section 2

1: The President shall be Commander in Chief of the Army and Navy of the United States, and of the Militia of the several States, when called into the actual Service of the United States; he may require the Opinion, in writing, of the principal Officer in each of the executive Departments, upon any Subject relating to the Duties of their respective Offices, and he shall have Power to grant Reprieves and Pardons for Offenses against the United States, except in Cases of Impeachment.

2: He shall have Power, by and with the Advice and Consent of the Senate, to make Treaties, provided two thirds of the Senators present concur; and he shall nominate, and by and with the Advice and Consent of the Senate, shall appoint Ambassadors, other public Ministers and Consuls, Judges of the Supreme Court, and all other Officers of the United States, whose Appointments are not herein otherwise provided for, and which shall be established by Law: but the Congress may by Law vest the Appointment of such inferior Officers, as they think proper, in the President alone, in the Courts of Law, or in the Heads of Departments.

3: The President shall have Power to fill up all Vacancies that may happen during the Recess of the Senate, by granting Commissions which shall expire at the End of their next Session.

Section 3

He shall from time to time give to the Congress Information of the State of the Union, and recommend to their Consideration such Measures as he shall judge necessary and expedient; he may, on extraordinary Occasions, convene both Houses, or either of them, and in Case of Disagreement between them, with Respect to the Time of Adjournment, he may adjourn them to such Time as he shall think proper; he shall receive Ambassadors and other public Ministers; he shall take Care that the Laws be faithfully executed, and shall Commission all the Officers of the United States.

Section 4

The President, Vice President and all civil Officers of the

United States, shall be removed from Office on Impeachment for, and Conviction of, Treason, Bribery, or other high Crimes and Misdemeanors.

Article III (Article 3 - Judicial)

Section 1

The judicial Power of the United States, shall
be vested in one supreme Court, and in such inferior Courts as the Congress may from time to time ordain and establish. The Judges, both of the supreme and inferior Courts, shall hold their Offices during good Behavior, and shall, at stated Times, receive for their Services, a Compensation, which shall not be diminished during their Continuance in Office.

Section 2

1: The judicial Power shall extend to all Cases, in Law and Equity, arising under this Constitution, the Laws of the United States, and Treaties made, or which shall be made, under their Authority;—to all Cases affecting Ambassadors, other public Ministers and Consuls;—to all Cases of admiralty and maritime Jurisdiction;—to Controversies to which the United States shall be a Party;—to Controversies between two or more States;—between a State and Citizens of another State;[10] — between Citizens of different States, —between Citizens of the same State claiming Lands under Grants of different States, and between a State, or the Citizens thereof, and foreign States, Citizens or Subjects.

2: In all Cases affecting Ambassadors, other public Ministers and Consuls, and those in which a State shall be Party, the supreme Court shall have original Jurisdiction. In all the other Cases before mentioned, the supreme Court shall have appellate Jurisdiction, both as to Law and Fact, with such Exceptions, and under such Regulations as the Congress shall make.

3: The Trial of all Crimes, except in Cases of Impeachment, shall be by Jury; and such Trial shall be held in the State where the said Crimes shall have been committed; but when not committed within any State, the Trial shall be at such Place or Places as the Congress may by Law have directed.

Section 3

1: Treason against the United States, shall consist only in levying War against them, or in adhering to their Enemies, giving them Aid and Comfort. No Person shall be convicted of Treason unless on the Testimony of two Witnesses to the same overt Act, or on Confession in open Court.

2: The Congress shall have Power to declare the Punishment of Treason, but no Attainder of Treason shall work Corruption of Blood, or Forfeiture except during the Life of the Person attainted.

Article IV (Article 4 - States' Relations)

Section 1

Full Faith and Credit shall be given in each State to the public Acts, Records, and judicial Proceedings of every other State. And the Congress may by general Laws prescribe the Manner in which such Acts, Records and Proceedings shall be proved, and the Effect thereof.

Section 2

1: The Citizens of each State shall be entitled to all Privileges and Immunities of Citizens in the several States.

2: A Person charged in any State with Treason, Felony, or other Crime, who shall flee from Justice, and be found in another State, shall on Demand of the executive Authority of the State from which he fled, be delivered up, to be removed to the State having Jurisdiction of the Crime.

3: No Person held to Service or Labour in one State, under the Laws thereof, escaping into another, shall, in Consequence of any Law or Regulation therein, be discharged from such Service or Labour, but shall be delivered up on Claim of the Party to whom such Service or Labour may be due.

Section 3

1: New States may be admitted by the Congress into this Union; but no new State shall be formed or erected within the Jurisdiction of any other State; nor any State be formed by the Junction of two or more States, or Parts of States, without the Consent of the Legislatures of the States concerned as well as of the Congress.

2: The Congress shall have Power to dispose of and make all needful Rules and Regulations respecting the Territory or other Property belonging to the United States; and nothing in this Constitution shall be so construed as to Prejudice any Claims of the United States, or of any particular State.

Section 4

The United States shall guarantee to every State in this Union a Republican Form of Government, and shall protect each of them against Invasion; and on Application of the Legislature, or of the Executive (when the Legislature cannot be convened) against domestic Violence.

Article V (Article 5 - Mode of Amendment)

The Congress, whenever two thirds of both Houses shall deem it necessary, shall propose Amendments to this Constitution, or, on the Application of the Legislatures of two thirds of the several States, shall call a Convention for proposing Amendments, which, in either Case, shall be valid to all Intents and Purposes, as Part of this Constitution, when ratified by the Legislatures of three fourths of the several States, or by Conventions in three fourths thereof, as the one or the other Mode of Ratification may be proposed by the Congress; Provided that no Amendment which may be made prior to the Year One thousand eight hundred and eight shall in any Manner affect the first and fourth Clauses in the Ninth Section of the first Article; and that no State, without its Consent, shall be deprived of its equal Suffrage in the Senate.

Article VI (Article 6 - Prior Debts, National Supremacy, Oaths of Office)

1: All Debts contracted and Engagements entered into, before the Adoption of this Constitution, shall be as valid against the United States under this Constitution, as under the Confederation.

2: This Constitution, and the Laws of the United States which shall be made in Pursuance thereof; and all Treaties made, or which shall be made, under the Authority of the United States, shall be the supreme Law of the Land; and the Judges in every State shall be bound thereby, any Thing in the Constitution or Laws of any State to the Contrary notwithstanding.

3: The Senators and Representatives before mentioned, and the Members of the several State Legislatures, and all executive and judicial Officers, both of the United States and of the several States, shall be bound by Oath or Affirmation, to support this Constitution; but no religious Test shall ever be required as a Qualification to any Office or public Trust under the United States.

Article VII (Article 7 - Ratification)

The Ratification of the Conventions of nine States, shall be sufficient for the Establishment of this Constitution between the States so ratifying the Same.

The Word "the", being interlined between

the seventh and eight Lines of the first Page, The
Word "Thirty" being partly written on an Erasure in
the fifteenth Line of the first Page. The Words "is tried" being
interlined between the thirty second and thirty third Lines of
the first Page and the Word "the" being interlined between
the forty third and forty fourth Lines of the second Page.

done in Convention by the Unanimous Consent of the States
present the Seventeenth Day of September in the Year of our
Lord one thousand seven hundred and Eighty-seven and of the
Independence of the United States of America the Twelfth **In
witness** whereof We have hereunto subscribed our Names,
George Washington, President and 39 others

Amendments

Bill of Rights

(The Preamble to The Bill of Rights)

Congress of the United States
    begun and held at the City of New-York, on Wednesday
the fourth of March, one thousand seven hundred and eighty
nine.

THE Conventions of a number of the States, having at the time of
their adopting the Constitution, expressed a desire, in order to

prevent misconstruction or abuse of its powers, that
further declaratory and restrictive clauses should be added: And as
extending the ground of public confidence in the Government,
will best ensure the beneficent ends of its institution.

RESOLVED by the Senate and House of Representatives of the
United States of America, in Congress assembled, two thirds of
both Houses concurring, that the following Articles be proposed
to the Legislatures of the several States, as amendments to the
Constitution of the United States, all, or any of which Articles,
when ratified by three fourths of the said Legislatures, to be valid
to all intents and purposes, as part of the said Constitution; viz.

ARTICLES in addition to, and Amendment of the <u>Constitution
of the United States of America</u>, proposed by Congress, and
ratified by the Legislatures of the several States, pursuant to
the fifth Article of the original Constitution.

(Articles I through X are known as the Bill of Rights)

Article the first. .... After the first enumeration required by the first
Article of the Constitution, there shall be one Representative for
every thirty thousand, until the number shall amount to one
hundred, after which, the proportion shall be so regulated by
Congress, that there shall be not less than one hundred
Representatives, nor less than one Representative for every forty
thousand persons, until the number of Representatives shall
amount to two hundred, after which the proportion shall be so
regulated by Congress, that there shall not be less than two

hundred Representatives, nor more than one Representative for
every fifty thousand persons.

Article the second. .... No law, varying the compensation for the
services of the Senators and Representatives, shall take effect, until
an election of Representatives shall have intervened. ^{see} <u>Amendment</u>
<u>XXVII</u>

Article [I] (Amendment 1 - Freedom of expression and religion)

Congress shall make no law respecting an establishment of
religion, or prohibiting the free exercise thereof; or abridging the
freedom of speech, or of the press; or the right of the people
peaceably to assemble, and to petition the Government for
a redress of grievances.

Article [II] (Amendment 2 - Bearing Arms)

A well regulated Militia, being necessary to the security of a free
State, the right of the people to keep and bear Arms, shall not be
infringed.

Article [III] (Amendment 3 - Quartering Soldiers)

No Soldier shall, in time of peace be quartered in any house, without the consent of the Owner, nor in time of war, but in a manner to be prescribed by law.

Article [IV] **(Amendment 4 - Search and Seizure)**

The right of the people to be secure in their persons, houses, papers, and effects, against unreasonable searches and seizures, shall not be violated, and no Warrants shall issue, but upon probable cause, supported by Oath or affirmation, and particularly describing the place to be searched, and the persons or things to be seized.

Article [V] (Amendment 5 - Rights of Persons)

No person shall be held to answer for a capital, or otherwise infamous crime, unless on a presentment or indictment of a Grand Jury, except in cases arising in the land or naval forces, or in the Militia, when in actual service in time of War or public danger; nor shall any person be subject for the same offense to be twice put in jeopardy of life or limb; nor shall be compelled in any criminal case to be a witness against himself, nor be deprived of life, liberty, or property, without due process of law; nor shall private property be taken for public use, without just compensation.

Article [VI] (Amendment 6 - Rights of Accused in Criminal Prosecutions)

In all criminal prosecutions, the accused shall enjoy the right to a speedy and public trial, by an impartial jury of the State and district wherein the crime shall have been committed, which district shall have been previously ascertained by law, and to be informed of the nature and cause of the accusation; to be confronted with the witnesses against him; to have compulsory process for obtaining witnesses in his favor, and to have the Assistance of Counsel for his defense.

Article [VII] (Amendment 7 - Civil Trials)

In Suits at common law, where the value in controversy shall exceed twenty dollars, the right of trial by jury shall be preserved, and no fact tried by a jury, shall be otherwise re-examined in any Court of the United States, than according to the rules of the common law.

Article [VIII] (Amendment 8 - Further Guarantees in Criminal Cases)

Excessive bail shall not be required, nor excessive fines imposed, nor cruel and unusual punishments inflicted.

Article [IX] (Amendment 9 - Unenumerated Rights)

The enumeration in the Constitution of certain rights, shall not be construed to deny or disparage others retained by the people.

Article [X] (Amendment 10 - Reserved Powers)

The powers not delegated to the United States by the Constitution, nor prohibited by it to the States, are reserved to the States respectively, or to the people.

Attest,

John Beckley, Clerk of the House of Representatives.

Sam. A. Otis Secretary of the Senate.

Frederick Augustus Muhlenberg Speaker of the House of Representatives.

John Adams, Vice-President of the United States, and President of the Senate.

(end of the Bill of Rights)

[Article XI] (Amendment 11 - Suits Against States)

The Judicial power of the United States shall not be construed to extend to any suit in law or equity, commenced or prosecuted against one of the United States by Citizens of another State, or by Citizens or Subjects of any Foreign State. *ratified #11   affects 10*

[Article XII] (Amendment 12 - Election of President)

The Electors shall meet in their respective states, and vote by ballot for President and Vice-President, one of whom, at least, shall not be an inhabitant of the same state with themselves; they shall name in their ballots the person voted for as President, and in distinct ballots the person voted for as Vice-President, and they shall make distinct lists of all persons voted for as President, and of all persons voted for as Vice-President, and of the number of votes for each, which lists they shall sign and certify, and transmit sealed to the seat of the government of the United States, directed to the President of the Senate;—The President of the Senate shall, in the presence of the Senate and House of Representatives, open all the certificates and the votes shall then be counted;—The person having the greatest number of votes for President, shall be the President, if such number be a majority of the whole number of Electors appointed; and if no person have such majority, then from the persons having the highest numbers not exceeding three on the list of those voted for as President, the House of Representatives shall choose immediately, by ballot, the President. But in choosing the President, the votes shall be taken by states, the representation from each state having one vote; a quorum for this purpose shall consist of a member or members from two-thirds of the states, and a majority of all the states shall be necessary to a choice. And if the House of Representatives shall not choose a President whenever the right of choice shall devolve upon them, before the fourth day of March next following, then the Vice-President shall act as President, as in the case of the death or other constitutional disability of the President. —The person having the greatest number of votes as Vice-President, shall be the Vice-President, if such number be a majority of the whole number of Electors appointed, and if no person have a majority, then from the two highest numbers on the list, the Senate shall choose the Vice-President; a quorum for the purpose shall consist of two-thirds of the whole number of Senators, and a majority of the whole number shall be necessary to a choice. But no person constitutionally ineligible to the office of President shall be eligible to that of Vice-President of the United States. *ratified #12*   *affects 8*

Article XIII (Amendment 13 - Slavery and Involuntary Servitude)

Neither slavery nor involuntary servitude, except as a punishment for crime whereof the party shall have been duly convicted, shall exist within the United States, or any place subject to their jurisdiction. *affects 11*

Congress shall have power to enforce this article by appropriate legislation. *ratified #13*

Article XIV (Amendment 14 - Rights Guaranteed: Privileges and Immunities of Citizenship, Due Process, and Equal Protection)

1: All persons born or naturalized in the United States, and subject to the jurisdiction thereof, are citizens of the United States and of the State wherein they reside. No State shall make or enforce any law which shall abridge the privileges or immunities of citizens of the United States; nor shall any State deprive any person of life, liberty, or property, without due process of law; nor deny to any person within its jurisdiction the equal protection of the laws.

2: Representatives shall be apportioned among the several States according to their respective numbers, counting the whole number of persons in each State, excluding Indians not taxed. But when the right to vote at any election for the choice of electors for President and Vice President of the United States, Representatives in Congress, the Executive and Judicial officers of a State, or the members of the Legislature thereof, is denied to any of the male inhabitants of such State, being twenty-one years of age, and citizens of the United States, or in any way abridged, except for participation in rebellion, or other crime, the basis of representation therein shall be reduced in the proportion which the number of such male citizens shall bear to the whole number of male citizens twenty-one years of age in such State. *affects 2*

3: No person shall be a Senator or Representative in Congress, or elector of President and Vice President, or hold any office, civil or military, under the United States, or under any State, who, having previously taken an oath, as a member of Congress, or as an officer of the United States, or as a member of any State legislature, or as an executive or judicial officer of any State, to support the Constitution of the United States, shall have engaged in insurrection or rebellion against the same, or given aid or comfort to the enemies thereof. But Congress may by a vote of two-thirds of each House, remove such disability.

4: The validity of the public debt of the United States, authorized by law, including debts incurred for payment of pensions and bounties for services in suppressing insurrection or rebellion, shall not be questioned. But neither the United States nor any State shall assume or pay any debt or obligation incurred in aid of insurrection or rebellion against the United States, or any claim for the loss or emancipation of any slave; but all such debts, obligations and claims shall be held illegal and void.

5: The Congress shall have power to enforce, by appropriate legislation, the provisions of this article. *ratified #14*

Article XV (Amendment 15 - Rights of Citizens to Vote)

The right of citizens of the United States to vote shall not be denied or abridged by the United States or by any State on account of race, color, or previous condition of servitude.

The Congress shall have power to enforce this article by appropriate legislation. *ratified #15*

Article XVI (Amendment 16 - Income Tax)

The Congress shall have power to lay and collect taxes on incomes, from whatever source derived, without apportionment among the several States, and without regard to any census or enumeration. *ratified #16*   *affects 2*

[Article XVII] (Amendment 17 - Popular Election of Senators)

1: The Senate of the United States shall be composed of two Senators from each State, elected by the people thereof, for six years; and each Senator shall have one vote. The electors in each State shall have the qualifications requisite for electors of the most numerous branch of the State legislatures. *affects 3*

2: When vacancies happen in the representation of any State in the Senate, the executive authority of such State shall issue writs of election to fill such vacancies: Provided, That the legislature of any State may empower the executive thereof to make temporary appointments until the people fill the vacancies by election as the legislature may direct. *affects 4*

3: This amendment shall not be so construed as to affect the election or term of any Senator chosen before it becomes valid as part of the Constitution. *ratified #17*

Article [XVIII] (Amendment 18 - Prohibition of Intoxicating Liquors)[16]

1: After one year from the ratification of this article the manufacture, sale, or transportation of intoxicating liquors within, the importation thereof into, or the exportation thereof from the United States and all territory subject to the jurisdiction thereof for beverage purposes is hereby prohibited.

2: The Congress and the several States shall have concurrent power to enforce this article by appropriate legislation.

3: This article shall be inoperative unless it shall have been ratified as an amendment to the Constitution by the legislatures of the several States, as provided in the Constitution, within seven years from the date of the submission hereof to the States by the Congress. *ratified #18*

Article [XIX] (Amendment 19 - Women's Suffrage Rights)

The right of citizens of the United States to vote shall not be denied or abridged by the United States or by any State on account of sex. *affects 15*

Congress shall have power to enforce this article by appropriate legislation. *ratified #19*

Article [XX] (Amendment 20 - Terms of President, Vice President, Members of Congress: Presidential Vacancy)

1: The terms of the President and Vice President shall end at noon on the 20th day of January, and the terms of Senators and Representatives at noon on the 3d day of January, of the years in which such terms would have ended if this article had not been ratified; and the terms of their successors shall then begin. *affects 5*

2: The Congress shall assemble at least once in every year, and such meeting shall begin at noon on the 3d day of January, unless they shall by law appoint a different day. *affects 5*

3: If, at the time fixed for the beginning of the term of the President, the President elect shall have died, the Vice President elect shall become President. If a President shall not have been chosen before the time fixed for the beginning of his term, or if the President elect shall have failed to qualify, then the Vice President elect shall act as President until a President shall have qualified; and the Congress may by law provide for the case wherein neither a President elect nor a Vice President elect shall have qualified, declaring who shall then act as President, or the manner in which one who is to act shall be selected, and such person shall act accordingly until a President or Vice President shall have qualified. *affects 9*   *affects 14*

4: The Congress may by law provide for the case of the death of any of the persons from whom the House of Representatives may choose a President whenever the right of choice shall have devolved upon them, and for the case of the death of any of the persons from whom the Senate may choose a Vice President whenever the right of choice shall have devolved upon them. *affects 9*

5: Sections 1 and 2 shall take effect on the 15th day of October following the ratification of this article.

6: This article shall be inoperative unless it shall have been ratified as an amendment to the Constitution by the legislatures of three-fourths of the several States within seven years from the date of its submission. *ratified #20*

Article [XXI] (Amendment 21 - Repeal of Eighteenth Amendment)

1: The eighteenth article of amendment to the Constitution of the United States is hereby repealed. *affects 16*

2: The transportation or importation into any State, Territory, or possession of the United States for delivery or use therein of intoxicating liquors, in violation of the laws thereof, is hereby prohibited.

3: This article shall be inoperative unless it shall have been ratified as an amendment to the Constitution by conventions in the several States, as provided in the Constitution,
within seven years from the date of the submission hereof to the States by the Congress. *ratified #21*

Amendment XXII (Amendment 22 - Presidential Tenure)

1: No person shall be elected to the office of the President more than twice, and no person who has held the office of President, or acted as President, for more than two years of a term to which some other person was elected President shall be elected to the office of the President more than once. But this article shall not apply to any person holding the office of President when this article was proposed by the Congress, and shall not prevent any person who may be holding the office of President, or acting as President, during the term within which this article becomes operative from holding the office of President or acting as President during the remainder of such term.

2: This article shall be inoperative unless it shall have been ratified as an amendment to the Constitution by the legislatures of three-fourths of the several states within seven years from the date of its submission to the states by the Congress. *ratified #22* _______

Amendment XXIII (Amendment 23 - Presidential Electors for the District of Columbia)

1: The District constituting the seat of government of the United States shall appoint in such manner as the Congress may direct: A number of electors of President and Vice President equal to the whole number of Senators and Representatives in Congress to which the District would be entitled if it were a state, but in no event more than the least populous state; they shall be in addition to those appointed by the states, but they shall be considered, for the purposes of the election of President and Vice President, to be electors appointed by a state; and they shall meet in the District and perform such duties as provided by the twelfth article of amendment.

2: The Congress shall have power to enforce this article by appropriate legislation. *ratified #23* _______

Amendment XXIV (Amendment 24 - Abolition of the Poll Tax Qualification in Federal Elections)

1. The right of citizens of the United States to vote in any primary or other election for President or Vice President, for electors for President or Vice President, or for Senator or Representative in Congress, shall not be denied or abridged by the United States or any state by reason of failure to pay any poll tax or other tax.

2. The Congress shall have power to enforce this article by appropriate legislation. *ratified #24* _______

Amendment XXV *affects 9* _______ (Amendment 25 - Presidential Vacancy, Disability, and Inability)

1: In case of the removal of the President from office or of his death or resignation, the Vice President shall become President.

2: Whenever there is a vacancy in the office of the Vice President, the President shall nominate a Vice President who shall take office upon confirmation by a majority vote of both Houses of Congress.

3: Whenever the President transmits to the President pro tempore of the Senate and the Speaker of the House of Representatives his written declaration that he is unable to discharge the powers and duties of his office, and until he transmits to them a written declaration to the contrary, such powers and duties shall be discharged by the Vice President as Acting President.

4: Whenever the Vice President and a majority of either the principal officers of the executive departments or of such other body as Congress may by law provide, transmit to the President pro tempore of the Senate and the Speaker of the House of Representatives their written declaration that the President is unable to discharge the powers and duties of his office, the Vice

President shall immediately assume the powers and duties of the office as Acting President.

Thereafter, when the President transmits to the President pro tempore of the Senate and the Speaker of the House of Representatives his written declaration that no inability exists, he shall resume the powers and duties of his office unless the Vice President and a majority of either the principal officers of the executive department or of such other body as Congress may by law provide, transmit within four days to the President pro tempore of the Senate and the Speaker of the House of Representatives their written declaration that the President is unable to discharge the powers and duties of his office. Thereupon Congress shall decide the issue, assembling within forty-eight hours for that purpose if not in session. If the Congress, within twenty-one days after receipt of the latter written declaration, or, if Congress is not in session, within twenty-one days after Congress is required to assemble, determines by two-thirds vote of both Houses that the President is unable to discharge the powers and duties of his office, the Vice President shall continue to discharge the same as Acting President; otherwise, the President shall resume the powers and duties of his office. *ratified #25*
___

Amendment XXVI (Amendment 26 - Reduction of Voting Age Qualification)

1: The right of citizens of the United States, who are 18 years of age or older, to vote, shall not be denied or abridged by the United States or any state on account of age. *affects 15*
___

2: The Congress shall have the power to enforce this article by appropriate legislation. *ratified #26*
___

Amendment XXVII (Amendment 27 - Congressional Pay Limitation)

No law varying the compensation for the services of the Senators and Representatives shall take effect until an election of Representatives shall have intervened. *ratified #27*